CATECHISM

in Conversation

SECOND EDITION

Linus Chua

Innovo
Publishing

Published by
Innovo Publishing, LLC
www.innovopublishing.com
1-888-546-2111

Innovo
Publishing

Providing Full-Service Publishing Services for
Christian Authors, Artists & Organizations: Hardbacks, Paperbacks,
eBooks, Audiobooks, Music & Videos

CATECHISM IN CONVERSATION

Biblical quotes are from The Holy Bible, King James Version.

ISBN 13: 978-1-936076-62-8
ISBN 10: 1-936076-62-4

Cover Design & Interior Layout: Innovo Publishing, LLC

Printed in the United States of America
U.S. Printing History

Second Edition: February 2011

Dedicated to my children:

Rebekah, Euan, and Luke.

May you grow up to know and love and live the truths
that are expressed in the Shorter Catechism.

Table of Contents

Foreword

There was a time when the Westminster Shorter Catechism was well known and highly regarded in Presbyterian churches and even in Calvinistic Baptist churches. Today, that is generally not so. In fact, a few years ago a pastor of a conservative Presbyterian Church saw me reading the Catechism and was so intrigued by it that he asked me where he could get a copy! In all his years of ministry, he apparently had only read about it in church history textbooks. I hold nothing against this pastor, but I was not only amazed but also saddened that the church should have allowed this diamond of a tool for Christian education to slip into oblivion while eagerly gorging on the trashy Sunday school materials that are being pandered everywhere.

I am convinced that this tragic lapse, together with the de-emphasis and even opposition to the use of the Confession of Faith, has led to the shallow and lawless brand of Christianity that characterises the life of so many professing Christians today.

Oh, may the Lord grant us His help that we may return to the old paths and walk in the way without being tossed to and fro by every wind of false doctrine and human opinion! Oh, that the Lord would restore our knowledge of His Word through the faithful and consistent use of the Catechism, which He has so kindly given us by His providence!

But first we must get the people interested in the Catechism again. How can we convince a people so accustomed to milk and porridge to taste and ingest the strong meat that we put in their hands?

This, I believe, is one of the things that this little book is seeking to do. And our brother has, in my opinion, done an excellent job at it. The Catechism is in itself crafted in such a way as to aid instruction through a catechetical or dialogical method, which has been used with much success by great teachers such as Plato, Anselm, Aquinas, and Gerstner. Our brother is essentially following this scholarly tradition. But he has dramatised it so engagingly, and has so seamlessly fitted the meaty statements of the Catechism into day-to-day conversation, that it will convince even the reluctant layperson that theology is not cold and heartless but rather thoroughly practical.

I found it very delightful, instructive, and refreshing to read this book. I am sure that in the hand of God it will be used to great profit to strengthen the faith of many and to restore the glory of Christ, which many a congregation has seen in better days. Amen.

JJ Lim
Pastor, Pilgrim Covenant Church
Singapore

Preface

Second Edition

It has been almost five years now since the first edition (2005) of *Catechism in Conversation* was published. Since then, I have received some helpful suggestions from various brethren and friends, and I have tried to incorporate as many of them into this new edition as possible.

One suggestion was to replace the somewhat archaic language of the Catechism's questions with more contemporary language. After some thought, I decided to leave the original questions unchanged because I would still like this book to be an introduction to the Westminster Shorter Catechism of 1647, so that anyone reading the book also would have read the entire catechism in its original form. However, in order the address the issue of archaism, I added introductory questions or comments to twenty-three of the questions in order to make the transition from contemporary to archaic language less abrupt. I also have added some illustrations to help make the conversations less dry at certain points.

Besides helpful suggestions, I have also received some encouraging remarks and comments. Here are four of them.

1. "Your kind gift of *Catechism in Conversation* arrived safely and in good shape and I wanted to say a hearty "thank you" for thinking of me. It looks to me like you have performed a "Thomas Watson" for modern folks! Thank you so much for such a useful tool." –Rev. Dr. Dale Ralph Davis, Presbyterian Church in America

2. "I have been enjoying your previous book on the catechism. Very nicely done. Very creative. I haven't finished it yet because one of our elders wanted to read it, so I will finish it when I get it back. Again, thank you." –Rev. Dr. Philip Kayser, Presbyterian Church in America

3. "Recommended Reading for those who want an easy way to remember the Shorter Catechism. The conversational style makes it easier to not only remember the questions and answers but Linus includes a dialogue which contains a simple explanation of each question and answer. Well thought out and written." –Rev. Dr. Donald J. Musin, Reformed Presbyterian Church General Assembly

4. "This is an unusual little book but very helpful. The author works his way through the Westminster Shorter Catechism as an imagined conversation between two men…The book is easily read and would make an excellent study for a young Christian." –Rev. William Macleod, Free Church of Scotland (Continuing)

It is my prayer and hope that this book might continue to be used by the Lord to introduce more Christians to the use of catechisms in general and the Westminster Shorter Catechism in particular.

Linus Chua,
Singapore, October 2010

Preface

First Edition

During my third year at college, I was introduced to the Westminster Shorter Catechism (WSC) by the man who is now presently my pastor. He gave me (and still gives me!) a lot of encouragement to study, and even to memorise, the entire Catechism! As I began to read it, I was fascinated by its content and structure; and I learnt a great deal from it too. So it was that one evening while walking back to my hostel from college, the idea of sharing with other Christians what I had recently discovered in the WSC came to my mind. I decided that writing a little book in conversational style, with all the Catechism's questions and answers incorporated, might be a good way to do it.

Some may already be asking, "What's a catechism?" Well, a catechism is simply a series of questions and answers that explain the basic principles of religion. It's a highly effective and useful tool that many pastors and parents in ages past have used to instruct their congregations and their children. Sadly, though, most churches today have altogether neglected the use of this tool, and many Christians are altogether ignorant of its existence. For this reason, I believe that there's once again a need to promote its use amongst Christian people today.

And why the Westminster Shorter Catechism? I believe that this catechism is one of the most accurate, faithful, and concise summaries of the Christian religion. Written in 1647 by the Westminster Assembly, this catechism was originally intended for children and those "of weaker capacity." Today, many of us may perhaps find it somewhat difficult to understand and use. It is my hope that this book will give us a little help in understanding its content and that we'll be encouraged to study it for ourselves in even greater detail.[1]

Besides encouraging Christians to use the Catechism, I hope that this book may also be a means of evangelism for those who are seeking to know more about Christianity. To all my unbelieving friends, I pray that you too may diligently seek the Lord while He may be found. And may your earthly journey end in the glories of heaven and in the presence of Jesus Christ!

Finally, may God be glorified, which is, after all, the chief end of all our reading and writing in this world.

Linus Chua
Singapore

Chapter 1

Man's Chief End (Q1)

It was late one Monday evening. The car came to a complete stop at the front porch. The eight-hour-long journey from Glasgow to London was finally over. Yet, although this particular journey had just ended, another one was about to begin. And it appears that this second "journey" will take a much longer time than the first.

THOMAS: That was some long drive! I'm certainly not going to try it again.

JONATHAN: Well, there's always a first time. I guess we'll be better off taking the train in the future.

TOM: Yes, we're definitely going to do that next time. But you know, Jon, while we were approaching our final service station stop, an unusual thought came to my mind, and it has been troubling me quite a bit ever since.

JON: Tell me about it.

TOM: At first, I was murmuring to myself about this seemingly endless journey and wondering when it would ever end. Then, suddenly, I thought about the time when you told me that our life in this world is just like a journey with a beginning and an ending. Now that is one "journey" I'm not keen on ending so soon!

JON: Is that what's troubling you – the ending of life's journey?

TOM: Yes. But more than that, I was also thinking about the purpose of our existence and the ultimate end of all life. You see, when we finally arrived in London, our journey ended and our purpose for the past eight hours of traveling was achieved. But I'm not so sure I know what my purpose in life's journey is. And when I finally reach the end of my life, will I have achieved this purpose? I was wondering, what is the chief goal in life? What – **What is the chief end of man?**

JON: Well Tom, I'm both surprised and pleased that you've asked this vital question. At least, it shows that you're on the right track. But I also must tell you that your question is a very profound one -- one that will inevitably lead to many more questions. In fact, it would seem like we're about to embark on yet another lengthy "journey," a "journey" with lasting consequences.

TOM: I didn't really expect my question to be *that* important. But please, carry on.

JON: **Man's chief end is to glorify God, and to enjoy Him forever.**

TOM: Hmmm—your answer is even more unexpected. Now I get what you meant when you said that my first question would lead to many more. In fact, I already have a couple of questions waiting for you!

JON: I'm sure you do, but first allow me to explain to you what I mean.

TOM: Go ahead.

JON: The purpose for man's existence is not actually found in man himself. If that were the case, my answer would have been something like, "Man's chief end is to glorify himself and to enjoy himself for as long as he lives." Instead, the purpose of our existence is found in God, who created us. We can achieve our chief end, which is to glorify and enjoy Him, only when our lives are God-centered and not man-centered.

TOM: Wait a minute; you're assuming that there is a God and that He created you for the purpose of glorifying and enjoying Him. In other words, this God you're talking about made everything in this entire universe, including man, and man can fulfill his chief end in life only if he glorifies and enjoys Him.

JON: Yes, that's right. Now I want you to assume that I'm right for the time being until I can show you more clearly the reason for my answer.

TOM: Assuming that you're right for the moment, tell me, what does it mean to glorify God?

JON: To glorify God is to reflect and to display to others the glory of God through our lives. It is to exalt His name in the world and magnify Him in the eyes of others. For example, if I say or do something that insults and dishonours Him, I'm not bringing Him glory. But if I speak the truth about God and do everything possible in my life to please God, then I will bring glory to Him. By believing in Him, obeying His commandments, and praising Him for who He is and for what He has done, I will glorify Him. A lot more can be said about glorifying God, but I think you get the idea.[2]

TOM: Hmm. I think so. How about enjoying God?

JON: Enjoying God can come only when we actively glorify Him. We enjoy Him by coming into His presence, listening to Him speak to us through His Word, speaking to Him in prayer, walking according to His Word, worshipping Him together with other Christians, and continuing in this close and happy relationship with Him throughout our lives.[3]

TOM: It seems as if enjoying God is something only you Christians can do.

JON: That's right! And that's because only Christians can bring glory to God in their lives. Non-Christians, while they are still without Christ, can never do anything to glorify God and consequently can never enjoy Him.

TOM: Earlier you mentioned that man's chief end is to glorify God and to enjoy Him **forever**. Tell me more about the implications of the word *forever*.

JON: Well, to a Christian, the end of life's journey on earth doesn't mark the end of his existence. In fact, physical death is just the stepping-stone to a far better life in the immediate presence of God. To be sure, a non-Christian continues to exist even after death too, but his condition will be infinitely different from that of a Christian. You see, in eternity a Christian continues to fulfill his chief end. After all, there can be no end to glorifying the infinitely glorious God. And there will be no end to enjoying His wonderful presence!

TOM: We started off by talking about the chief aim and purpose for living. I must admit that you seem to know what you're talking about, even though you haven't as yet proven anything. I must remind you that you'll still need to show me that God exists and that this God indeed created man to glorify and enjoy Him forever.

JON: Well, I'll be most happy to do so, but I think it's getting late and we're both pretty tired. Let's continue this interesting conversation tomorrow.

TOM: I look forward to that. Good night, Jon.

JON: Good night, Tom.

Chapter 2

The Word of God (Q2-3)

A t breakfast the next morning...

JONATHAN: We left off last night on the point about God's existence and His purpose for creating man.

THOMAS: I'm glad you didn't forget about it. I was beginning to wonder if you were trying to evade my question yesterday by calling it a night!

JON: No, Tom, I haven't forgotten. But I must confess that this is not the easiest of topics to deal with, and you may take a while to come to see my point of view. Before we talk about the existence of God, I would like first of all to deal with the matter of *revelation,* or the way in which God reveals Himself to man. There are essentially two ways, namely, natural revelation and special revelation. Natural revelation refers --

TOM: Pardon my interrupting, but I think I know your reason for dealing with revelation before actually talking about the existence of God. If God really exists, He would most probably want to communicate with His creatures. And if we know for sure the right way in which He communicates with us, then this inevitably will lead us back to Him and establish His existence without a doubt. Not only will we know that He exists; there is also a high possibility that we would know what He is like and what He requires of us.

JON: Tom, you've really made my task much easier! And you're right, the question of how we know and especially how we know God is extremely important. Okay, then, let's talk about the two ways in which God reveals Himself to man. First, there is natural revelation. This refers to God revealing Himself to us through nature. In the Bible, the psalmist says in Psalm 19:1, "The heavens declare the glory of God; and the firmament sheweth his handiwork." Again, in Romans 1:20, Paul writes, "For the invisible things of him [God] from the creation of the world are clearly seen, being understood by the things that are made, *even* his eternal power and Godhead; so that they are without excuse:" These verses in fact tell us that we are without any excuse if we do not acknowledge that God exists, because the world that we are living in contains more than sufficient evidence of the Creator God.

TOM: Talking about creation, not too long ago, I was thinking about the "big bang" theory and the theory of evolution. I came to the conclusion that there has to be another explanation for the existence of the universe in general and of life in particular. It is absolutely impossible for something to come out of nothing. To say that "Chance + Time + Space = Universe" is ridiculous.[4] It would be similar to saying something like, "Nothing + Nothing + Nothing = Everything"! After all, chance, time, and space have no causal or creative powers in themselves, and adding them all up won't help. Well, perhaps you are right. It does seem easier to believe that some greater being made this universe, instead of attributing it to evolution. What about the second mode of revelation?

JON: Special revelation refers to God revealing Himself to man through His Word. For Christians, we believe that the Bible alone is the Word of God. It is infallible, inerrant, and sufficient because it's from God. In other words, the Bible is all we really need to direct us to God, and we can be sure that it makes no mistakes at all since it comes from one who makes no mistakes. This is what the Bible claims for itself: "All scripture is given by inspiration of God, and is profitable for doctrine, for reproof, for correction, for instruction in righteousness: That the man of God may be perfect, throughly furnished unto all good works" (2 Timothy 3:16-17).

TOM: I can agree that the Bible claims to be the Word of God, but how do I know that such a claim is true? What evidence can you give me that the Bible is in fact God's Word?

JON: That's a good question, Tom. Let me simply say this: THE Bible is a very unique book. First, it is unique in its consistency and continuity. Here is a book written over a period of 1600 years by over 40 different authors from various walks of life, including kings, fishermen, poets, statesmen, scholars, and peasants, and under very different circumstances. Yet, the authors never contradicted each other. All that the Bible says is accurate and true. In fact, there is an amazing harmony and continuity throughout its pages. Second, it is unique in its circulation. The Bible has been read by more people and published in more languages than any other book in all of human history. Have you ever wondered why this is so? Third, it is unique in its content. No mere human author could have written such a profound and majestic book. And certainly no mere human being could make that many prophecies that have been fulfilled (there are over 300 Old Testament prophecies fulfilled with the coming of Christ and the New Testament age). When the Bible predicts something, it is as good as done! Finally, the Bible is unique in its life-changing effects on people who have read and believed it.

TOM: Sounds impressive, but I'm not totally convinced.[5]

JON: I would highly recommend that you pick up the Bible today and start reading it for yourself. Many people foolishly deny that the Bible is the Word of God before they even read it for themselves. A book of such great importance in human history deserves to be read at least once by everyone!

TOM: Okay, I'll do just that. Which book of the Bible should I start with?

JON: Start with the Gospel according to Luke.[6]

TOM: Thanks. So far, we've talked about the way God reveals Himself to man and about the Bible. But my mind keeps going back to what you said last night about the chief end of man. Assuming that all you've said so far is true, I was wondering how God, who created man, actually directs him so that he achieves his purpose in life. **What rule hath God given to direct us how we may glorify and enjoy him?**

JON: **The Word of God, which is contained in the Scriptures of the Old and New Testaments, is the only rule to direct us how we may glorify and enjoy him.**

TOM: I should have guessed it! If the Bible is indeed the Word of God, then surely it will direct and guide us so that if we truly and fully follow it, we will be able to achieve the purpose for which God has created us. I'd like to ask another question before we finish breakfast and go to work.

JON: Go ahead.

TOM: I would like to find out what the Bible is basically all about. Or to be a little more specific, **what do the Scriptures principally teach?**

JON: **The Scriptures principally teach what man is to believe concerning God, and what duty God requires of man.** You see, the Bible is not some science or history textbook that you turn to when you need to study for an examination. In fact, the Bible doesn't tell us all the information we might like to know about this universe. But the Bible teaches us the most important and fundamental things we need to know in life and that we can't find anywhere else. It teaches us all the essential truths we must know and believe about God. This is important because, after all, no one can truly worship and serve a God he doesn't know. However, having a sound knowledge and faith in God is not all. We also need to know and obey His commandments to us. We will glorify and enjoy God only when we truly believe in Him and diligently obey His commandments.

TOM: Thanks for the helpful summary of the Bible. I'll bear that in mind whenever I read it. See you later this evening.

Chapter 3

God (Q4-6)

A fter dinner on a bright summer evening…

THOMAS: Jon, how about taking a stroll along the river Thames for some fresh air?

JONATHAN: Sounds great to me.

A little while later, our friends are sitting by the river Thames just outside the Royal Festival Hall.

TOM: I was in Blackwell's during lunchtime and I noticed that there were quite a number of books under the "Religion" section of the bookshop. There are literally hundreds of religions in this world right now and thousands more throughout human history. Do you think that religion is another possible evidence for the existence of God?

JON: I certainly think so. Throughout history, man has always sought after a god whom he can bow down to and worship. In all civilizations, whether ancient and primitive, or modern and advanced, you will find some form of religion present. The reason is simple: Man, unlike animals or other living creatures, has the capacity and desire to worship something. This aspect of man hasn't changed since the beginning of his existence. God, who created man, gave him this capacity and desire.

TOM: During my college days, I once heard an atheistic philosopher remark, "I am very sure that God does not exist. But the one thing that vexes me no end is the fact that countless people throughout the ages have always been worshipping some form of deity."

JON: I guess this philosopher doesn't understand that his dilemma can be easily resolved if he would just admit that some form of deity does indeed exist!

TOM: Granted that God does exist, could you kindly define in simple terms, **what is God?**

JON: **God is a Spirit, infinite, eternal, and unchangeable, in His being, wisdom, power, holiness, justice, goodness, and truth.**

TOM: Now that's quite a mouthful. I hardly consider that a simple definition!

JON: It'll help if we look at this definition in three parts. First, the phrase "God is a Spirit" tells us about the nature of His being. He is an immaterial substance, which cannot be seen, felt, weighed, or measured. Unlike man, God does not have a physical body. Now it is very difficult to give a precise definition of a spirit. There is an element of mystery here that we cannot fully understand but we must nevertheless believe, because Jesus Himself taught this truth (John 4:24). Second, God is infinite, eternal, and unchangeable. These three attributes set God apart from everything else. Earlier when I used the phrase "a Spirit," I was in fact saying that God is not the only spirit. Angels are also called spirits (Hebrews 1:14). Besides, man has a body and a spirit too. But when I say that God is infinite, eternal, and unchangeable, I'm speaking about the attributes or characteristics of God that are unique to Him alone. To be sure, angels are far superior to human beings in terms of their knowledge, strength, and abilities. But because angels, like men, are created beings, they too are finite, temporal, and changeable. God, however, is not limited at all by time, space, or circumstances. He has no beginning and no ending, and He does not change at all.

TOM: God certainly sounds great!

JON: You're right. The psalmist says in Psalm 48:1, "Great is the LORD, and greatly to be praised." Third, we deal with the communicable attributes of God. By communicable attributes, I mean those attributes that man can experience, understand, and possess, howbeit in a very limited way. Well, we could spend many days just discussing God's awesome power, perfect justice, absolute truth, marvelous goodness, and so on. Perhaps we'll leave that to some other time. Meanwhile, I think you can begin to appreciate why Christians spend so much time praising and exalting the God they worship.[7]

CATECHISM IN CONVERSATION

TOM: I guess so. But I've got another question. How many Gods are there in this universe? **Are there more Gods than one?**

JON: **There is but one only, the living and true God.**

TOM: Does the Bible say so?

JON: Yes, it does. In fact, no truth is more persistently and emphatically taught in the Bible than this. For example, Isaiah 45:5 says, "I *am* the LORD, and *there is* none else, *there is* no God beside me." And Jeremiah 10:10 says, "But the LORD *is* the true God, he *is* the living God, and an everlasting king:"

TOM: Earlier you mentioned Jesus Christ. Is He also God, and if so, then **how many persons are there in the Godhead?**

JON: Yes, He is God. **There are three persons in the Godhead: the Father, the Son, and the Holy Ghost; and these three are one God, the same in substance, equal in power and glory.**

TOM: Sounds pretty confusing. Are you saying something like, 1+1+1=1 and 3 at the same time and in the same relationship?

JON: No, not at all. You see, to say, 1+1+1=1 and 3 at the same time is both illogical and nonsensical. If a certain doctrine is true, it will always stand up logically as well as theologically. Yet, having said that, I must say that the doctrine of the Trinity is another sacred mystery that man in his finite mind can't fully comprehend. Still, the scriptural fact remains: though there is but one living and true God who cannot be divided, there are three persons in the Godhead (Father, Son and Holy Spirit), each fully and equally God, and these three persons are distinguished from each other.[8]

TOM: Can you give an illustration of the Trinity?

JON: I'm afraid the doctrine of the Trinity is without analogy and every illustration (and there have been many attempts to illustrate it throughout the ages) will be defective in one way or another. In fact, the moment we try to illustrate it, we either *add* something to what the Bible teaches, or *subtract* from it, or else say something that is totally *different*; and none of these things is acceptable!

TOM: How important is the doctrine of the Trinity?

JON: Very! For example, no one can be a true Christian if he does not believe that Jesus Christ is God. Also, many cults and heresies arose from a wrong understanding of this doctrine. For example, the Jehovah's Witnesses reject this doctrine and claim that Jesus Christ is not actually God but a created being. To them, only the Father (Jehovah) is God. Then there are the polytheists, who believe that more than one being may be called "god"; they do not believe that these "gods" have one identical essence or substance of being. The Mormons are one such example.

TOM: Thanks. I'll think about all that we've discussed today.

JON: Glad to hear that. Well, let's get home before the sun sets!

Chapter 4

The Works of God (Q7-11)

Some weeks have passed since their last conversation. Today is a bank (public) holiday, and our friends are once again free to speak with each other at length.

THOMAS: Does it ever bother you that so much in life is beyond our control? For example, we have no real control over nature. There is no stopping a hurricane or a volcanic eruption or an earthquake from occurring. And if a huge asteroid in our solar system "decided" to come crashing into our planet, we couldn't do very much to stop it. And there are a hundred and one diseases and accidents that could strike us at anytime without warning and give us an early end to life's journey!

JONATHAN: I guess I'm not very conscious of these things until they happen, or at least threaten to happen! Sometimes, it helps to be ignorant of the potential dangers around us, doesn't it? In fact, many people live in a state of denial and choose to think that such things won't ever happen to them.

TOM: I suppose denial is one way out. But then again, it's not all that reassuring or comforting, is it? How about the God we discussed some weeks ago? Does He have anything to do with all this?

JON: Oh, yes, He certainly does. The attributes of God, which we briefly talked about last time, and the works of God are closely related. In other words, who God is and what He does can't be separated.

TOM: What are the works of God?

JON: Before we can answer that, we must talk about God's decrees (or His purposes). You see, God doesn't do anything without first planning for it before hand.

TOM: Okay, then, **what are the decrees of God?**

JON: **The decrees of God are His eternal purpose, according to the counsel of His will, whereby, for His own glory, He hath foreordained whatsoever comes to pass.**

TOM: Are you telling me that everything that ever happened, is happening, or will happen in this universe has been planned beforehand by God and that nothing can ever change His plans?

JON: Yes, that's right, and that's consistent with the nature of God. If God is eternal, His plans must be from all eternity. If God is unchanging, then His plans cannot change. If God is all-powerful, all wise, and all good, then His plans must be the best of all. God doesn't need to consult anyone or get anyone's approval before He does something. He does everything for His own glory. Now, although God is all-knowing, He doesn't decree something because He knew beforehand what would happen. Instead, things happen simply because He planned it to happen!

TOM: Your statement about God's decrees sounds logical, but it does raise two problems. First, if God ordains everything that happens, then isn't He the author of evil, or what you Christians would call sin? Second, if God ordains all things, then what about man's free will and responsibility? Isn't it destroyed?

JON: Tom, I must say that you're pretty sharp today! To answer your first question -- yes, God ordained sin. He certainly could have stopped it, but He didn't. Instead, He allowed it to enter His creation. But having said that, I must say this: God is by no means the author of sin. The Bible states this very clearly (1 John 1:5; James 1:13). Furthermore, God never permits or allows anything to come to pass that He does not also overrule for His own glory and for the good of His people. As to your second question -- no, man's responsibility is not destroyed or diminished because of God's decrees. God still holds man responsible for his choices and his actions. Each person acts freely and always chooses according to his natural inclinations. God never forces anyone to do anything. It's helpful to distinguish between the first cause and the secondary cause. God is the first and ultimate cause of everything, while man is responsible for secondary causes. Yet, God does not normally control the affairs of man apart from secondary causes; or, in other words, God does not decree the end apart from the means. He has ordained that the end shall be accomplished by means of the means! I must admit that beyond this, I can't really explain much further.[9]

TOM: And I must say that I can't accept the idea that God has foreordained everything from eternity including man's decisions and actions. Perhaps we can look into this question of God's sovereignty and man's responsibility in more detail in the future. But meanwhile, I'm interested in knowing how God carries out His plans. **How doth God execute His decrees?**

JON: **God executeth his decrees in the works of creation and providence.**

TOM: You mentioned two things in your answer – creation and providence. **What is the work of creation?**

JON: **The work of creation is, God's making all things of nothing, by the word of His power, in the space of six days, and all very good.** If you have seriously thought about God's work of Creation, you realise how wonderfully amazing it is. God made everything out of nothing and with the use of nothing but His spoken Word. As human beings, we are limited by space and time. We can't imagine a time when there was no "time"! And we can't fathom how "space" can be created without the existence of space to start with! Furthermore, when God created everything, He created it all very good, and He did it within a span of six days.[10]

TOM: From the way I see it, the most important work of God's Creation is none other than man himself, but **how did God create man?**

JON: **God created man male and female, after his own image, in knowledge, righteousness, and holiness, with dominion over the creatures.** When we talked about the chief end of man, I said that man was created to glorify God by reflecting His glory in this world. There is in every person an image or a stamp of God upon that person. In other words, we all bear a certain resemblance and likeness to our Creator. We possess knowledge, righteousness, and holiness in a limited way, while our Creator possesses these attributes to an infinite degree. Also, we note that God, who rules over the whole universe, created man to be the head over all the creatures and all of creation on earth.

TOM: How about the second way in which God executes His decrees? **What are God's works of providence?**

JON: **God's works of providence are, his most holy, wise, and powerful preserving and governing all his creatures, and all their actions.** God not only creates, but He also sustains and maintains His creation. He didn't create the universe and then leave it alone to run its own course. Just as God was actively involved in the initial work of Creation, so also is He actively involved in running the universe. If God stops preserving this universe for just one second, it would immediately cease to exist. And not only does God control nature, but He also controls the activities of man. For example, God rules over the nations and kingdoms. The Bible, in Daniel 4:25, says, "The most High ruleth in the kingdom of men, and giveth it to whomsoever he will." He appoints the times of kings and maps out the boundaries of their kingdoms.

TOM: In other words, you are saying that nothing happens by chance and that everything, whether due to natural or human causes, is under the sovereign control of God.

JON: That's right. Well, now that you know about God's providence and His eternal decrees, does that give you a little more comfort and assurance when you are faced with so much uncertainty in life?

TOM: I guess it should -- but only if I'm really sure that God is on my side!

JON: But why shouldn't God be on your side? In other words, why should God be against you or anyone else for that matter?

Chapter 5

The Fall of Man (Q12-15)

TOM: I'm not so sure. Perhaps something happened after God created man that caused man's relationship with God to be "strained."

JON: Go on. I think you're getting somewhere.

TOM: Man was created very differently from the rest of the animals and the rest of creation. If God made man to be so different and special, perhaps God required something special from him.

JON: Yes, when God first created man, He did something very different from the rest of creation. God breathed into his nostrils the breath of life, and man became a living soul. Now if God acted in a very special way towards man in His work of Creation, wouldn't He also act in a very special way towards man in His work of providence?

TOM: I don't see why not. **What special act of providence did God exercise towards man in the estate wherein he was created?**

JON: **When God had created man, he entered into a covenant of life with him, upon condition of perfect obedience; forbidding him to eat of the tree of the knowledge of good and evil, upon the pain of death.**

TOM: Am I right to say that when God made Adam, He entered into a relationship with Adam such that if Adam obeyed God perfectly, he would enjoy God's reward, and if he disobeyed God, he would suffer grave consequences?

JON: Yes, you've got it. But I would like to add a few more things. First, we must remember that God was under no obligation to enter into such a covenant with man. And neither was God obliged to reward Adam, even if Adam obeyed God perfectly. It was Adam's duty to obey his Creator. Second, God was absolutely sovereign when He made this covenant. God and God alone decided the terms of the covenant, that is, the conditions, the rewards, and the punishments. Third, we see the great grace of God in this covenant. Man, of his own, could never do anything to earn or merit God's gift. If God gave anything at all, it would be solely because He is a gracious God. Last, the conditions in this covenant of life were very favourable for Adam. If Adam disobeyed, it would be entirely his fault.

TOM: So did Adam and Eve keep to their part of the covenant? **Did our first parents continue in the estate wherein they were created?**

JON: **Our first parents, being left to the freedom of their own will, fell from the estate wherein they were**

created, by sinning against God. Perhaps the greatest tragedy in all of human history occurred when man fell. God created man in a state of innocence, but man chose to fall from that state by sinning against God. Did you notice the phrase "freedom of their own will"? This tells us that there was once a time when man had both the *liberty* and the *ability* to obey or disobey God's commandments. But after the fall, man lost his ability to obey God perfectly. Although he is still at liberty to choose whether to do good or evil, he has lost that ability to do good. From that time, all he ever chooses to do is evil in God's sight.

TOM: You mentioned "sinning against God." I understand that to mean a failure to meet certain standards. But I would like a more precise definition of it. **What is sin?**

JON: **Sin is any want of conformity unto, or transgression of, the law of God.** From this, we learn that there are two aspects to sin. First, "want of conformity unto the law of God" refers to the sin of omission. This simply means not doing something that we're supposed to do. For example, if God commands us to worship Him and we don't, then we have sinned against Him. Second, "transgression of the law of God" refers to the sin of commission. If I do something I'm not supposed to do, I have also sinned. Some common examples would be stealing, lying, and murdering. We must remember that sin is judged according to God's standard, not man's.

TOM: I think I understand what sin is.

JON: Now it's my turn to ask you a question. What was the sin of Adam and Eve in the fall, or **what was the sin whereby our first parents fell from the estate wherein they were created?**

TOM: **The sin whereby our first parents fell from the estate wherein they were created, was their eating the forbidden fruit.** In other words, Adam and Eve transgressed the law of God and committed the sin of commission.

JON: Excellent. I couldn't have said it better myself!

Chapter 6

The Consequences of the Fall (Q16-19)

THOMAS: The fall of man certainly sounds serious. Maybe we also should talk about the consequences of the fall. What was the extent of the fall in mankind, or to put it simply, who was involved in it? **Did all mankind fall in Adam's first transgression?**

JONATHAN: **The covenant being made with Adam, not only for himself, but for his posterity; all mankind, descending from him by ordinary generation, sinned in him, and fell with him, in his first transgression.** The extent of the fall was total. Every one after Adam was affected. When God made that covenant of life with Adam, He was actually making a covenant with the entire human race. Adam acted as the representative head of all mankind. And so when Adam sinned, the whole human race sinned in Adam and fell with Adam.

TOM: Pardon me for being a little rude, but I don't think God is very fair when He judges the entire human race in one single person – Adam. Perhaps if someone else stood in Adam's place, that person wouldn't have done what Adam did, and all mankind wouldn't have fallen. Also, why was the covenant made with the whole human race and not with individuals?

JON: Of course God could have done it differently, but He didn't. Let's start with your second objection about why God doesn't deal with us as individuals in this covenant. We must remember that the entire human race is just like one big family with a common father – Adam. In most families, the head of the family represents the rest of the household in making important decisions within the family and in dealing with any external problems. Another analogy I can think of would be that of a country. When a country is dealing with another country, it sends a representative to negotiate on behalf of the whole nation. So you see, this idea of "one representing many" isn't a new or strange one after all, is it?

TOM: I guess it isn't. But how about my first objection regarding the selection of that representative? Why did Adam have to be the one and not someone else?

JON: Why not? After all, it was God who chose Adam. God's choice, given the character of God, must surely have been the best one. But even if you could choose your own representative, there would be no guarantee that he or she wouldn't fall like Adam did. Furthermore, remember that Adam was a perfectly perfect man, unlike any of us. And if he could fall, I don't think any of us, being so imperfect, would dare say that we could have done better ourselves.

TOM: I'm not quite ready to accept this covenant or representative idea as yet, although I can see that it does makes quite a bit of sense. But moving on, what were the consequences of the fall? **Into what estate did the fall bring mankind?**

JON: **The fall brought mankind into an estate of sin and misery.** After Adam fell, all of us who came after him were born into a sinful and miserable condition.

TOM: So the two consequences arising from the fall are sin and misery. Let's talk about the first one. **Wherein consists the sinfulness of that estate whereinto man fell?**

JON: **The sinfulness of that estate whereinto man fell consists in the guilt of Adam's first sin, the want (lack) of original righteousness, and the corruption of his whole nature, which is commonly called original sin; together with all actual transgressions which proceed from it.**

TOM: I observe four elements in your statement about the sinful estate into which mankind has fallen: first, the guilt of Adam's first sin; second, the lack of original righteousness; third, the corruption of the whole nature; and, fourth, actual transgressions.

JON: Very good. Actually if you think about it carefully, this sinful estate can be divided into just two parts, namely, the sin of our nature and the sin of our lives. All of us are sinners by nature and sinners in practice. The first three elements you mentioned come under the sin of our nature, while the fourth element refers to the sin of our lives. Earlier, we talked about how Adam represented us in the covenant of life and how we too share in the guilt of Adam's sin. Furthermore, man, who was created after the image of God in righteousness, has now lost this original righteousness.

TOM: What does the "corruption of his whole nature" mean?

JON: This tells us about the extent of the corruption within us. Every part of our lives has been corrupted and infected with the disease of sin. We are corrupted in our outward as well as our innermost parts. No part of us is left untouched by this radical corruption of our nature. It is only by God's providence that we are kept from working out our sinful nature to its full extent.

TOM: To summarise this point on the sinfulness of man's condition – man is sinful by nature and therefore he sins. Also, even if a person never actually committed a single sin in his life, he would still be guilty because of his relationship with Adam.

JON: That's right.

TOM: How about the second consequence of the fall? **What is the misery of that estate whereinto man fell?**

JON: **All mankind by their fall lost communion with God, are under his wrath and curse, and so made**

liable to all miseries in this life, to death itself and to the pains of hell forever. We were originally created to enjoy God. Sadly, after the fall, we were cut off from God and were no longer able to enjoy His close presence and sweet fellowship. Not only that, but we also have become the enemies of God and are subjects of His great wrath because of our sin. All the miseries you see in this world, including death itself, can be traced back to the fall. And the greatest misery of all, which we don't see with our physical eyes, awaits us when we die -- an eternity in hell!

TOM: All this sure sounds like bad news for mankind! Somehow, although your description of the sinfulness of man's estate made me a little uneasy, it was your statement about the miseries of the fall that really made me uncomfortable.

JON: Why is that so?

TOM: You see, it is possible for a person to deny the reality of sin. For example, I can choose not to believe that Adam's fall was also my fall and that all my actual sins are not as bad as you make them out to be. But while I may try to deny the sinfulness of sin, I cannot deny the reality of the miseries in this life and of death itself. Every single day without fail, I see or hear about people suffering and dying all over the world. Up until today, no one has ever given me a reasonable answer for the cause of all this misery! But now, all of a sudden, it seems to make perfect sense. The miseries in this life are a direct result of the fall of man and sin. Now if God is real, and I'm beginning to think that He is, then He sure feels very far away from me. I feel as if I've offended Him and that He is my enemy. And to make matters worse, the threat of spending an eternity in hell really frightens me!

Chapter 7

God's Redemption Plan (Q20-22)

After a few moments of silence…

THOMAS: Jon, I've got an important question to ask you: **Did God leave all mankind to perish in the estate of sin and misery?**

JONATHAN: Thank God, the answer is no! **God having, out of his mere good pleasure, from all eternity, elected some to everlasting life, did enter into a covenant of grace, to deliver them out of the estate of sin and misery, and to bring them into an estate of salvation by a Redeemer.**

TOM: I can't think of anything more wonderful than what you've just said! If there is anything that I would call good news, it has to be this – that God didn't leave all mankind to perish forever in their sin and misery but provided a way of salvation. God is truly gracious!

JON: I'm thrilled to hear that. In fact, I'm often saddened to know that many Christians themselves aren't half as excited about this good news as you are. They've forgotten that God could have left them alone to perish everlastingly, but He didn't. Instead, He saved them from their sinful and miserable condition. In this second covenant, that is, the covenant of grace, God did everything for His people. He chose them from among many millions, not because they were so good or deserved to be saved, but purely out of His great grace. And He saved them by providing a Redeemer, who perfectly satisfied all the conditions of the covenant on their behalf.

TOM: Why didn't God choose to save everyone instead of just the elect?

JON: I really don't know, but I know that this is what the Bible teaches. Ephesians 1:5 says that God "predestinated us unto the adoption of children by Jesus Christ to himself, according to the good pleasure of his will." God, who is sovereign, is free to do whatsoever He pleases. While we're on this earth, we'll never be able to comprehend why God chooses some to be saved and allows the rest to perish, except that in doing so He is greatly glorified. Perhaps a better question to ask would be, "Why does God choose to save anyone in the first place?"[11]

TOM: I guess you're right. God is not obliged to save even a single person, since everyone has sinned against Him.

JON: Listen to this statement written by a group of godly Christian leaders many years ago: "The doctrine of this high mystery of predestination is to be handled with special prudence and care. ... So shall this doctrine afford matter of praise, reverence, and admiration of God, and of humility, diligence, and abundant consolation to all that sincerely obey the gospel" (Westminster Confession of Faith, chapter 3).

TOM: That's a lovely statement! Earlier, you mentioned the term *Redeemer*. What does it mean?

JON: Well, to redeem is to buy back something that was once yours. The word for *Redeemer* in Hebrew (the original language of the Old Testament) signifies a person of very close relation who has the right to redeem a mortgage.

TOM: **Who is the Redeemer of God's elect?**

JON: **The only Redeemer of God's elect is the Lord Jesus Christ, who, being the eternal Son of God, became man, and so was, and continueth to be, God and man in two distinct natures, and one person, forever.** There are two things to note. First, the word "only" is very important. Acts 4:12 has this to say about Jesus, "Neither is there salvation in any other: for there is none other name under heaven given among men, whereby we must be saved." Christ is the only way of salvation. Just as Adam was the only representative of mankind in the first covenant, so also is Christ the only representative of His people in the second covenant. This is why Christ often is referred to by theologians as the Second Adam. And just as the covenant of life was made primarily with Adam, so also is the covenant of grace made primarily with Christ. Second, we must acknowledge that Jesus is both God and man at the same time. His two natures -- the divine nature and the human nature -- are distinct from each other. Yet they are both found in one and the same person. To say that Jesus was not fully God is erroneous; likewise to say that Jesus wasn't actually a man also is false. Like the doctrine of the Trinity, the doctrine of the two natures of Christ is not something our finite minds can fully understand.

TOM: Hmm, I'll need to think more about this unique idea of a dual and distinct nature united in a single person. But tell me more about this unique individual. **How did Christ, being the Son of God, become man?**

JON: **Christ, the Son of God, became man, by taking to himself a true body, and a reasonable soul, being conceived by the power of the Holy Ghost, in the womb of the virgin Mary, and born of her, yet without sin.**

TOM: What significance does the phrase "a true body and a reasonable soul" have?

JON: A "true body" means that while Jesus was on earth, He took to Himself the same kind of body that you and I possess. His body was made of flesh and blood, and He felt hunger, thirst, pain, and tiredness, just as we do. A "reasonable soul" refers to Christ having a human soul contained in a human body just like us. Some people think that the divine nature of Christ took the place of the human soul; but that is an error, for if Christ did not have a human soul, then He would not be fully human. We read in the Scriptures that Jesus wept, sorrowed, and even increased in wisdom. Now God does not weep, sweat, get hungry, or grow in wisdom, but Christ, who is the God-man, does. As an aside, when Christ died on the cross, He did so as the God-man, although strictly speaking, death belongs to His human and not divine nature, for if His divine nature had died, the whole universe would have ceased to exist that very moment!

TOM: Why does Christ, the Redeemer, need to be God and man at the same time?

JON: Christ is the Mediator between God and man. A mediator is a middle person who makes up the breach between two disagreeing parties. God and man were separated at the fall, but Christ came to mediate and reconcile man to God through His precious blood. It is important that this Mediator be very God Himself, because the task of redemption is so great that only He is able and qualified to do it. Yet at the same time, this Mediator must also be a man, because it is man who needs salvation, and redemption can be accomplished only through the obedience of a man.

TOM: I think I get it. The Redeemer or Saviour of mankind must be able to reach both God and man at the same time. And Christ alone is able to do this because He is both God and man, in two distinct natures and one person, forever.

JON: Very good. Well, we have covered a lot of ground in our discussion today. We've talked about the works of God, the fall of man, the consequences of the fall, and, finally, God's plan of redemption. All this has led you to acknowledge that God is real, that man is a sinner, and that Jesus Christ is the only Saviour of the world. But until and unless Christ becomes your personal Saviour and Lord, this knowledge is of little use.

TOM: Jon, indeed we've talked about many wonderful and fascinating things today. I guess I'll need a little more time to ponder and reflect upon them. But if I may ask one more question, "What must I do to be saved?"

JON: Believe in the Lord, and you shall be saved (Acts 16:31a).

TOM: But how? I don't seem to have the faith to believe in the Lord right now. I -- I am unable to believe.

JON: Tom, salvation is of the Lord. Only those whom God sovereignly regenerates will ever be saved. And only those who are thus regenerated will have true faith. There is nothing you can do to save yourself. But that doesn't mean that you sit still and do nothing. On the contrary, you must diligently seek the Lord for salvation. Christ tells us to seek and strive to enter into that narrow gate of salvation (Luke 13:24). Read God's Word diligently each day. Pray earnestly and persistently to the Lord for saving faith to believe in Him. Repent of your sins, and do all that is in your power to keep sin out of your life; but most importantly, come to church every Sunday to listen to the preaching of God's Word. And continue doing these things until God takes away your heart of stone and gives you a heart of flesh. As you seek the Lord for salvation, be encouraged that all who truly seek Him will find Him, or rather be found of Him. Jeremiah 29:13 says, "And ye shall seek me, and find me, when ye shall search for me with all your heart."

TOM: Thanks for the encouragement.

Chapter 8

The Work of Christ our Redeemer (Q23-28)

Almost a month has passed. Today is Sunday, or the Lord's Day, as Christians call it. Our friends have just come back from church and are sitting in their garden, enjoying a cup of tea.

THOMAS: I really enjoyed the psalms we sang this morning during the worship service, especially the 110th Psalm.

JONATHAN: Yes, the words of that psalm speak wonderfully of Christ as our great Lord.

The Lord did say unto my Lord, Sit thou at my right hand,
Until I make thy foes a stool, whereon thy feet may stand.
The Lord shall out of Sion send the rod of thy great pow'r:
In midst of all thine enemies be thou the governor.
A willing people in the day of pow'r shall come to thee,
In holy beauties from morn's womb;

Thy youth like dew shall be.
The Lord himself hath made an oath,
and will repent him never,
Of th' order of Melchisedec thou art a priest for ever.[12]

TOM: According to the pastor, this psalm describes Christ as being both a king and a priest. I wonder if He has any other duties or functions in relation to His work as Redeemer. **What offices doth Christ execute as our Redeemer?**

JON: **Christ, as our Redeemer, executeth the offices of a prophet, of a priest, and of a king, both in his estate of humiliation and exaltation.**

TOM: I think it's pretty important to know what each of these three offices are about, so that we'll be able to better understand and appreciate the work of Christ as Redeemer. Let's talk about the first office you mentioned – prophet. **How doth Christ execute the office of a prophet?**

JON: **Christ executeth the office of a prophet, in revealing to us, by his Word and Spirit, the will of God for our salvation.** A prophet is a special person appointed by God to speak to the people on His behalf and reveal to them His will. During Old Testament times, God raised up many prophets to preach His word. Yet, they did not speak by their own authority or wisdom. Rather it was the Spirit of Christ that spoke through them (1 Peter 1:11). When Christ came into this world, He was the fulfillment of all the Old Testament prophecies concerning the Messiah. In fact, Christ Himself was the Prophet promised by God in the Old Testament (Deuteronomy 18:15, Acts 3:22). And He came to teach us the way of salvation.

TOM: But how does Christ speak to us today?

JON: In two ways – externally through His Word and internally by His Spirit. The Bible we hold in our hands is the very Word of Christ to us. If we neglect it or treat it lightly, we will surely perish. On the other hand, just reading it with our own human understanding is not enough to make us wise unto salvation. We need the Spirit of Christ to teach us and illuminate our minds so that we'll understand and believe the deep and sacred things of God. Both of these are very important and necessary to us if we are to be saved.

TOM: **How doth Christ execute the office of a priest?**

JON: **Christ executeth the office of a priest, in his once offering up of himself a sacrifice to satisfy divine justice, and reconcile us to God; and in making continual intercession for us.** A prophet is one who represents God before man. A priest, on the other hand, does the opposite; he represents man before God. The duties of a priest in the Old Testament involved offering sacrifices and praying for the people. Now when Christ came, He did infinitely more than any priest had previously done. He offered Himself as a sacrifice by dying on the cross to atone for the sins of His people.

TOM: Is there any other way for Christ to save His people other than dying on the cross for them?

JON: There is no other way. You see, the only way for God's perfect justice to be satisfied and for sinful man to be reconciled to Him was for Christ to die on the cross. Sin cannot be put away without the shedding of blood. And only the Lord Jesus, who was perfectly righteous and without sin, could do this work. As Christ hung on the cross, He bore the wrath and curse of God on His people for their sins. In this way, their debt of sin was forever cancelled.

TOM: What does Christ do in the work of intercession?

JON: Christ presents the merit of His blood to the Father and, in virtue of the price paid, pleads for mercy on behalf of His people. Christ is like an advocate for the sinner before the judge. And upon Christ's plea, God pardons the sinner. When Satan, the accuser, comes before God to bring a charge against a believer, Christ by His intercession answers all his accusations. Satan never succeeds when he tries to accuse a child of God. The Bible says, "Who shall lay any thing to the charge of God's elect? … It is Christ that … maketh intercession for us" (Romans 8:33-34).

TOM: **How doth Christ execute the office of a king?**

JON: **Christ executeth the office of a king, in subduing us to himself, in ruling and defending us, and in restraining and conquering all his and our enemies.** The Lord Jesus is known by the title "King of kings and Lord of lords" (Revelation 19:16). You can think about the duties of a king in two parts – first, in dealing with his own subjects and, second, in dealing with his enemies. First, as King, Christ gives His people laws to obey and directions to follow. And He enables His subjects to obey Him by taking away their sinful heart and giving them a new heart of obedience (Ezekiel 36:26-27). Christ also will preserve, support, and strengthen His people when they undergo sufferings and temptations. Second, as King, He will restrain His enemies from hurting His people so that all things will work for His glory and for their good. Ultimately, Christ will conquer and punish all those who oppose Him and His people.

TOM: It seems to me that there are only two kinds of people in this world -- the people of God and the enemies of God.

JON: You're absolutely right. Those who are not for the Lord are against Him. There is no neutral ground as far as our relationship with God is concerned.

TOM: Earlier you mentioned that Christ is a prophet, a priest, and a king, both in His estate of humiliation and exaltation. Let's talk about the two states of Christ – humiliation and exaltation. **Wherein did Christ's humiliation consist?**

JON: **Christ's humiliation consisted in his being born, and that in a low condition, made under the law, undergoing the miseries of this life, the wrath of God, and the cursed death of the cross; in being buried,**

and continuing under the power of death for a time. Can you identify the eight steps involved in the humiliation of Christ?

TOM: I'll try. First, in entering human nature; second, in assuming a low position; third, in being subject to the law; fourth, in suffering the miseries of life; fifth, in suffering the wrath of God; sixth, in being crucified on the cross; seventh, in being buried; and, eighth, in remaining in the grave for three days.

JON: You've got it! But you know, it's very hard for us to appreciate the full extent of Christ's humiliation. It is no small matter at all for the infinite God to take the form of a finite man. Furthermore, when Christ was on this earth, He didn't occupy a high and mighty position but lived as a poor man of no reputation. And though He was the giver of the law, He was willing to subject Himself to the law and to obey it perfectly. As a man, He suffered hunger, pain, sorrow, and poverty. And His suffering reached its pinnacle when He took upon Himself the sins of the world and experienced the full wrath of God against sin. In fact, we are told that He was made a curse for His people (Galatians 3:13). Even the angels on high must have been filled with surprise and amazement when they saw the eternal Son of God suffering all these things.

TOM: No wonder Christians are always full of thanksgiving for all that Christ has done for them. How about the exaltation of Christ? **Wherein consisteth Christ's exaltation?**

JON: **Christ's exaltation consisteth in his rising again from the dead on the third day, in ascending up into heaven, in sitting at the right hand of God the Father, and in coming to judge the world at the last day.** This time there are just four steps involved in Christ's exaltation. Can you identify them?

TOM: First, in rising from the dead; second, in ascending up to heaven; third, in sitting at the right hand of God; and, last, in coming to judge the world some day.

JON: That's right, and I think you now know why Christians are always praising and exalting the Lord Jesus Christ![13]

TOM: I guess I do. In fact, the 110th Psalm has become that much more meaningful!

Chapter 9

The Spirit's Work in Redemption (Q29-31)

THOMAS: The work of Christ in redemption is truly a great work, but how is it actually applied to us? **How we are made partakers of the redemption purchased by Christ?**

JONATHAN: **We are made partakers of the redemption purchased by Christ, by the effectual application of it to us by his Holy Spirit.** God's plan of salvation is a wonderful plan involving all three persons of the Godhead. God the Father gave His Son to be the Saviour of the world. God the Son purchased this redemption by His perfect obedience, and God the Holy Spirit, who proceeds from both the Father and the Son, applies redemption to the experience of believers and puts them in actual possession of it.

TOM: Is the Holy Spirit's work absolutely necessary? And if so, why?

JON: Yes, the Holy Spirit's work in redemption is absolutely necessary. The reason is simple. Fallen men are by nature dead in sin (Ephesians 2:1). John Bunyan, the author of *The Pilgrim's Progress,* once said, "When God came to man to convert him, he found him a dead man."[14] Bunyan of course was talking about the spiritual condition of an unbeliever. And so, before a person is sensible to the things of God and able to respond to Him, the Holy Spirit must first work in that person's heart and quicken it.

TOM: How does He do that? **How doth the Spirit apply to us the redemption purchased by Christ?**

JON: **The Spirit applieth to us the redemption purchased by Christ, by working faith in us, and thereby uniting us to Christ in our effectual calling.** Christ's purchased redemption becomes ours by our union with Him. In this union, we are spiritually and inseparably joined to Christ, who is our Head. The way in which we are united to Christ is by faith, and the faith that we have is a result of the Spirit's work in us.

TOM: Wait a minute, you've lost me this time.

JON: I think it'll help if we think in terms of the logical order or steps of salvation. First, the Spirit effectually calls. Then, the sinner responds in faith, and finally he is united to Christ.

TOM: That sounds a little better, but **what is effectual calling?**

JON: **Effectual calling is the work of God's Spirit, whereby, convincing us of our sin and misery, enlightening our minds in the knowledge of Christ, and renewing our wills, he doth persuade and enable us to embrace Jesus Christ, freely offered to us in the gospel.** Can you spot the four steps in the effectual call of the Spirit?

TOM: First is convincing a person of sin, second is opening his eyes to the truth of the gospel, third is inclining his will and desire towards God, and fourth is persuading and helping him to receive Jesus Christ.

JON: You're spot on!

TOM: It seems to me that effectual calling is something that happens inside rather than outside a person. Is that right?

JON: That's right. It's useful to distinguish between the external or outward call and the internal or inward call. We find the external call of God in the preaching of the gospel. When the gospel is preached, everyone who hears it is called to come to Christ. But, sadly, we find that many who hear this call do not respond to it because of the hardness of their hearts. On the other hand, the inward call is an effectual call because all whom God calls inwardly certainly will respond to Christ in faith. Romans 8:29-30 teaches us this wonderful truth. In fact, this passage often has been called the golden chain of salvation. Could you read it for us?

TOM: "For whom he did foreknow, he also did predestinate *to be* conformed to the image of his Son, that he might be the firstborn among many brethren. Moreover whom he did predestinate, them he also called: and whom he called, them he also justified: and whom he justified, them he also glorified" (Romans 8:29-30). I assume that the call in this passage refers to the inward and effectual call of God.

JON: Yes, that's right! It has to be the inward, effectual call because *all* whom God calls He justifies, and *all* whom God justifies He also glorifies. Working backwards – just as it is impossible for God not to glorify someone whom He justifies, so also is it impossible for God not to justify someone whom He calls. Now, usually when God calls a person inwardly, He also calls that person outwardly by means of the preaching of the gospel. Perhaps a good illustration of effectual calling can be seen in the raising of Lazarus from the dead (John 11). Lazarus had been dead for four days already. He was not able to hear or do anything because he was dead. No amount of persuasion, pleading, or even threatening by any person could make Lazarus come out. Yet when the Lord Jesus went up to his grave and spoke in a loud voice, "Lazarus, come forth," Lazarus indeed obeyed and came out of his grave. Just as the Lord gave Lazarus the power to hear His voice, so also the Holy Spirit gives His elect (and no one else!) the ability to hear and the willingness to obey the outward call of the gospel.

TOM: I've been reading the Gospel of John this past week, and I came across chapter 11 a few days ago. This parallel between physical and spiritual quickening is very helpful indeed.

JON: I'm glad you've been reading your Bible. Keep it up! Earlier I mentioned John Bunyan and his book *The Pilgrim's Progress.*[15] This is a timeless classic, and I recommend it to you.

TOM: I'll definitely get a copy and start reading it as soon as possible.

JON: Okay. We had better pack up and get going, or we'll be late for the evening service.

Chapter 10

The Benefits of Redemption (Q32-38)

E arly the next morning…

THOMAS: Jon, something very strange and wonderful happened last night.

JONATHAN: What was it?

TOM: Just before going to bed, I experienced a rather strange feeling deep within my heart. It's difficult to describe. The verse that the pastor preached on last evening kept ringing in my ears -- Isaiah 45:22: "Look unto me, and be ye saved, all the ends of the earth: for I *am* God, and *there is* none else." And for once in my life, I truly believed those words. It was as if my eyes were opened and my heart was made sensible to spiritual things. I felt the awful, crushing load of sin in my life, and I realised my great need to turn to Christ and to rest on Him alone for salvation. I knew I had to come to Christ and receive Him on His terms as He is offered to me in the gospel. I wanted Christ to be my Prophet – to teach me and guide me in the way of salvation. I wanted Him to be my Priest – to cleanse me from all my sins by His precious blood, to reconcile me to God, and to make continual intercessions at the right hand of the Father for me. I wanted Him to be my King – to rule over every area of my life.

JON: Then what did you do?

TOM: I wept before the Lord and pleaded with Him to be my Redeemer and to save me from my sins. I felt a deep love for Him after that and was filled with gratitude for what He had done for me. Jon, I wonder if what happened last night was for real. I wonder if my conversion experience was genuine and I have truly embraced Christ.

JON: Tom, only God knows whether you are truly a child of His or not. But from what you've said, I'd be surprised if your conversion is anything less than genuine! I truly praise and thank the Lord for showing such great grace and mercy towards you. May the Lord richly bless you and keep you as you travel along this narrow path that leads to life. Remember that the full assurance of salvation is ultimately not something that I or anyone else can give to you. It is the gift of God to all His children who are living in obedience to His Word (Romans 8:15-16). Continue to study the Scriptures diligently, and seek the Lord often in prayer. Join fellow Christians regularly for worship and fellowship. Labour and strive for the evidences of salvation in your life. As 2 Peter 1:10 says, "Wherefore the rather, brethren, give diligence to make your calling and election sure." And Philippians 2:12 tells us, "Work out your own salvation with fear and trembling." Finally, I'll like to recommend yet another book to you: *A Sure Guide to Heaven* by Joseph Alleine.[16] This is an excellent book about conversion, and I'm sure you'll find it helpful.

TOM: Thanks for all your encouragement and help! We talked about the Spirit's work in redemption yesterday, and how He applies redemption to a person. If you can spare some time today, I'd love to find out more about the benefits of redemption.

JON: I'll be more than happy to do so. After all, what could be a more suitable topic than this to talk about right now?

TOM: Let's begin with the benefits of redemption in this life. **What benefits do they that are effectually called partake of in this life?**

JON: **They that are effectually called do in this life partake of justification, adoption, and sanctification, and the several benefits which, in this life, do either accompany or flow from them.** There are three primary or essential benefits: justification, adoption, and sanctification, together with several other secondary benefits, which we'll come to later.

TOM: Just a minute; let me write these words down: jus-ti-fi-ca-tion, a-dop-tion, sanc-ti-fi-ca-tion. Wow, that's thirteen syllables in three words! Okay, let's tackle the first one first. **What is justification?**

JON: **Justification is an act of God's free grace, wherein he pardoneth all our sins, and accepteth us as righteous in his sight, only for the righteousness of Christ imputed to us, and received by faith alone.** When a person is justified before a holy God, he is declared to be righteous in His sight. The problem is that no man is righteous in and of himself. If ever anyone is to be justified, he has to be made righteous by God Himself. And God does it by imputing our guilt to Christ on the cross and at the same time imputing the righteousness of Christ to us. This is what theologians call double imputation. I prefer to call it the Great Exchange! Justification is an act of God's free grace precisely because we didn't do anything to deserve it.

TOM: If the basis of justification is the righteousness of Christ, then why do Christians speak of justification by faith alone? Shouldn't it be justification by the righteousness of Christ?

JON: Strictly speaking, we are justified by the righteous works of Christ. However, when we speak of justification by faith alone, we are talking about the instrument rather than the ground or basis of justification. Faith is like the hand that reaches out to receive the gift. And faith is not considered a good work because it is a gift of God (Ephesians 2:8). No man is ever justified by his own works. Instead, we are justified by Christ's work through the instrument of faith. In other words, faith is merely the *instrumental* cause, while the righteous works of Christ is the *meritorious* cause of our justification. It's important to understand this because many Christians today think that their faith actually merits justification![17]

TOM: I'll be careful to watch out for that error. Next, **what is adoption?**

JON: **Adoption is an act of God's free grace, whereby we are received into the number, and have a right to all the privileges of the sons of God.**

TOM: Adoption is certainly an easier concept to understand than justification. I'm sure that even little children are able to understand it without too much difficulty. However, I did notice one similarity between the two – both justification and adoption are acts of God, which imply that both are done by God all at once.

JON: Yes, that's right. But notice that adoption logically follows justification. We were all once sinful creatures, enemies of God and children of the devil. It is only when we are made righteous through Christ that God receives us into His family and makes us His sons. We are given the title "son of God" and enjoy all the privileges that the sons of God have. We can come before our heavenly Father freely, without fear that He will cast us away from His presence. We enjoy the Father's protection and provision throughout our life and have the assurance that He will work all things for our good (Romans 8:28).

TOM: **What is sanctification?**

JON: **Sanctification is the work of God's free grace, whereby we are renewed in the whole man after the image of God, and are enabled more and more to die unto sin, and live unto righteousness.** Justification and adoption are solely the acts of God. But here, we observe that sanctification, which logically follows justification and adoption, involves both the work of God and the work of man. In other words, man, by God's grace, has an active role to play in his own sanctification. After God regenerates us, we are enabled by His Holy Spirit to live a holy life. Although we'll never be perfect in this life, with each passing day, we are transformed more and more into the image of Christ as we put to death our sinful members and put on righteousness. Thus, sanctification is a gradual and ongoing process that begins at regeneration and ends when we die.

TOM: Why is it necessary for a Christian to undergo this process of sanctification? Can a person be saved and not sanctified?

JON: There are two common mistakes that people make about sanctification. First, there are some who teach that a person must first be sanctified before he can be justified. This leads to a form of justification by works, which we have shown to be false. Second, there are those who believe that sanctification is optional in salvation. They claim that as long as a person is saved, it doesn't really matter how he lives his life after that. This leads to what we call "easy believism," or antinomianism. Both of these mistakes are fatal and have resulted in many sincere but false converts. Sanctification is important because it is God's will for us (1 Thessalonians 4:3). God saves us from sin so that we can now live a righteous life. Without sanctification, there is no evidence of our justification. In other words, a person who calls himself a Christian but continues living in sin is most probably not saved in the first place.

TOM: I get it; you can't have salvation without sanctification, because justification, adoption, and sanctification are all absolutely essential elements in salvation. No one can be saved without these benefits, and only those who enjoy these benefits are truly saved!

JON: That's absolutely right!

TOM: Earlier you mentioned that besides these three primary benefits, there are also some secondary benefits. What are they? **What are the benefits which in this life do accompany or flow from justification, adoption, and sanctification?**

JON: **The benefits which in this life do accompany or flow from justification, adoption, and sanctification, are, assurance of God's love, peace of conscience, joy in the Holy Ghost, increase of grace, and perseverance therein to the end.** Here are five benefits that accompany or flow from the first three essential ones. While it is not possible for a person to be saved without justification, adoption, and sanctification, it is quite possible that a true Christian may not experience all these secondary benefits at all times.

TOM: Can you think of any of these benefits that may be absent from a true believer?

JON: Let's take the assurance of God's love for example. A new believer may not fully understand or experience this assurance until some time later. This is consistent with what I mentioned earlier about how all Christians should actively work out their salvation with fear and trembling and should give diligence to making their calling and election sure. Another example of this is when a Christian sins against the Lord. We read in the Scriptures of how godly men lost their joy and peace as a result of their sin. When we sin against the Lord, we grieve His Holy Spirit and consequently cannot expect to enjoy "peace of conscience" or "joy in the Holy Ghost."

TOM: What does "increase of grace" and "perseverance therein to the end" mean?

JON: To increase in grace is to grow in the grace and knowledge of Jesus Christ (2 Peter 3:18). As we grow in grace, we will increase in our love for the Lord and for His Word. We will hate sin with increasing hatred and strive to put it out of our lives. Our faith will grow, and we will demonstrate more and more of the fruit of the Spirit, such as love, joy, peace, long-suffering, goodness, and so on (Galatians 5:22-23). "Perseverance to the end" means that all true believers will continue in a state of grace and salvation till they leave this earth, because the Lord certainly will keep His people safe and secure. He will preserve them so that none will ever be lost (John

10:28). Just as we have been saved by God's grace, we will also be preserved by His grace to the end of life's journey.

TOM: Thus far, we've been talking about the benefits of redemption that are enjoyed in this life. Are there any benefits to be enjoyed after one leaves this life? **What benefits do believers receive from Christ at death?**

JON: **The souls of believers are at their death made perfect in holiness, and do immediately pass into glory; and their bodies, being still united to Christ, do rest in their graves till the resurrection.** Death brings a person into an intermediate state. This intermediate state stands between his present state and his final or eternal state. When a Christian dies, his soul is immediately perfected in holiness and brought into the very presence of God in heaven, while his body rests in the grave, awaiting the resurrection at the last day. At the resurrection, he will be given a glorious and renewed body.

TOM: So you're saying that for a Christian, death is simply the separation of his soul, which goes to heaven, from his body, which remains on earth for a time until the resurrection.

JON: That's right. But on the other hand, when an unbeliever dies, his soul goes straight to hell, while his body remains on earth. And at the resurrection, both soul and body will be united again, and cast into hell to suffer eternal punishment there. No wonder our Lord Jesus warns us in Matthew 10:28 to fear God rather than man, because whereas evil men are only able to kill the body and not the soul, God is able to destroy both body and soul in hell.

TOM: What a contrast there is between a believer and an unbeliever! Now I know why you mentioned some months ago that the unbeliever's condition in eternity will be very different from the believer's. One last question before we end: **What benefits do believers receive from Christ at the resurrection?**

JON: **At the resurrection, believers being raised up in glory, shall be openly acknowledged and acquitted in the day of judgment, and made perfectly blessed in the full enjoying of God to all eternity.** If death is the separation of an imperfect body from an imperfect soul, then resurrection, for a Christian, is the union of a perfected soul with a perfected body. Now immediately after the resurrection, there will be a great day of judgment. Every person who ever lived will stand before Christ, the righteous Judge, for judgment; and He will judge all people according to their deeds. That will be a very dreadful day for all unbelievers as they face God's wrath. But for believers, Christ shall openly acknowledge us before the whole world to be His very own people. And we shall glorify and enjoy Him forever and ever.

TOM: The benefits of redemption, which Christ has purchased for us, are truly wonderful. How I look forward to the full enjoyment of each one of them both in this life and in the life to come! And thank you for taking the time through all these months to explain these important truths about the Christian faith.

JON: Well, it's been a great joy to be of help to you. Up until today, we have discussed what man is to believe concerning God. From here, we should move on to talk about what duty God requires of man. Let's set aside some time each week to do a more systematic study of this important topic of man's duty towards God. How about Friday evening?

TOM: That'll be great! Do you think I could invite a friend to join us as well?

JON: Sure! See you on Friday then.

Chapter 11

The Moral Law of God (Q39-44)

Friday evening 7:30 p.m. (week 1)

THOMAS: Jon, I would like you to meet my good friend Sarah.

JONATHAN: Hello, Sarah. Glad to meet you. It's good that you can join us in our study. I'm sure Tom has told you by now what we'll be doing for the next ten weeks or so.

SARAH: Yes, he has. In fact, I was quite excited when he invited me to this weekly discussion and told me what the two of you intend to do. You see, I was brought up in a Christian home and went to Sunday school at an early age. But throughout all these years, I've never actually had the opportunity of doing a study of say the Ten Commandments or the Lord's Prayer.

CATECHISM IN CONVERSATION

JON: That's not surprising. Many Sunday school children these days are made to memorise such familiar Bible passages without being taught what they mean. Then, later on in life, they begin to realise that these so-called familiar passages aren't that familiar after all, because they never understood them in the first place! Well, I don't promise that we'll cover these topics in great detail. But I hope that our study will be enough to give us a basic understanding of what God requires of man.

TOM: Let's begin then. My first question has to do with the duty and obligation that God has placed upon man. **What is the duty which God requireth of man?**

JON: **The duty which God requireth of man, is obedience to his revealed will.** A true believer will not only believe all the doctrines of God in His Word; he also will strive to obey all His commandments. Faith and obedience (or good works) must always go together.[18] In fact, James says that "faith without works is dead" (James 2:20). By that he means that true faith will never fail to result in good works. Obedience to God's will is an evidence of a true and living faith.

SARAH: It's clear that before we can obey, we need to know what it is that we must obey. So my question is, **What did God at first reveal to man for the rule of his obedience?**

JON: **The rule which God at first revealed to man for his obedience, was the moral law.** Our obedience to God must correspond with His word, and in particular,

82

the moral law. The Puritan Thomas Watson said, "To seem to be zealous, if it be not according to the word, is not obedience, but will-worship."[19]

TOM: But what is the moral law?

JON: The moral law is the expression of God's will for mankind. It is founded upon the very nature and character of God. By obeying the moral law, we actually reproduce God's image in this world. Before Adam fell, mankind had no need for the moral law to be written out externally because it was already written in their hearts, and it was perfectly obeyed. But after the fall, the moral image of God in man was badly defaced and marred, and thus he needed the moral law to show him what he was supposed to do right from the beginning.

TOM: So the moral law reveals something of God's character to us. Where can we go to find a summary of the moral law, or **where is the moral law summarily comprehended?**

JON: **The moral law is summarily comprehended in the Ten Commandments.** Sarah, you've been going to church since you were very young. What are your views on the Ten Commandments?

SARAH: Well, many of the Old Testament laws are no longer applicable to Christians today, although some of them still are. Just recently, a friend of mine told me that Christians are not obliged to observe every one of the Ten Commandments because not all of them are moral in nature. Frankly, I'm a little confused. How do we know which of the laws are relevant to us today and which aren't? I've also heard of people who say that we don't need to observe the entire law (including the Ten Commandments) nowadays because the law was given to the nation of Israel and not to us. They claim that we are now living in the dispensation of grace and that the law of God has been done away with the coming of Christ and replaced by a new set of commandments. What, then, should our attitude be towards the law of God in the Old Testament and in particular, the moral law, or the Ten Commandments?

JON: It's sad to hear that many sincere Christians today are sincerely wrong in their understanding of God's law, and as a result of that, they do not live lives that please and glorify God. In fact, many of them are guilty of what Thomas Watson calls "will-worship," that is, worshipping and serving God according to their own will rather than God's will. Let's try to get a better understanding of the law of God. First, we should recognise that the entire Old Testament law generally can be divided into three categories: ceremonial law, judicial law, and moral law. First, the ceremonial laws (e.g., animal sacrifices, observance of special feasts or days) have been done away under the New Testament, because these served as types and shadows of the coming Christ. And since Christ has come, there is no longer a need for them. In fact, it would be a great sin and a denial of Christ to reintroduce them. Second, the judicial or civil laws (e.g., dealing with cases of adultery, divorce, perjury), were given by God for the government of the people of Israel as the Old Testament church, or church under-age. These laws expired together with the state of that people. The church today, unlike in Old Testament days, is no longer limited to any particular nation or land, and so these laws, in terms of their outward form, are no longer binding on us. Nevertheless, the substance or underlying principles of those laws continue to be applicable even today.[20] Third, we have the moral law, which is still very relevant to us. Does anyone have any idea why this is so?

SARAH: Well, if the moral law of God is founded upon the moral character of God, then surely it must be perpetual and universal, because God's character is perfect and unchanging. For example, in the ninth commandment, God forbids lying because He is a God of truth and He hates falsehood (John 14:6; Hebrews 6:18; James 1:17; Proverbs 6:16-17, 19). Since the law of God doesn't change, we can presume that it continues to apply unless God tells us otherwise. After all, God is the giver of the law, and only He has the right to change its administration. And since there's no place in all of Scripture that teaches us that God has abrogated His moral law, or the Ten Commandments, it must still be applicable to us today.

JON: Very good! I'd like to add two other points. First, the moral law provides us with the only true definition of sin. First John 3:4 tells us that "sin is the transgression of the law." Paul says in Romans 4:15, "For where no law is, there is no transgression." If we can somehow explain away the law, we will be left with no reliable standard to measure sin and to determine right and wrong. At best, we are left with a serious case of moral relativism! Second, when God gave us the moral law, He spoke all the Ten Commandments audibly and wrote them on two tables of stone with His finger. He then instructed His people to place these two tables of stone in the ark of the covenant, which represented the very presence of God in their midst. Listen to the words of Moses in Deuteronomy 4:12-13, reminding the people of what happened at Mount Sinai when he received the law from God: "And the LORD spake unto you out of the midst of the fire: ye heard the voice of the words, but saw no similitude; only ye heard a voice. And he declared unto you his covenant, which he commanded you to perform, even ten commandments; and he wrote them upon two tables of stone." Notice that there are *ten* and not nine or eight commandments. It is not up to us to pick or choose which ones we want to obey and which we want to do away with!

TOM: Looks like we can't run away from keeping the Ten Commandments! But what is the essence of them? **What is the sum of the Ten Commandments?**

JON: **The sum of the Ten Commandments is, To love the Lord our God with all our heart, with all our soul, with all our strength, and with all our mind; and our neighbour as ourselves.** Some people have the wrong idea that there is a basic conflict between law and love. They don't realise that all the law and the prophets are actually based on these two commandments -- to love God and to love man.

SARAH: Are you saying that the Ten Commandments are really ten rules for expressing and demonstrating our love to God and man?

JON: Exactly! And as we study each commandment in detail, we'll begin to see this more clearly.

TOM: I'm getting more and more excited about these Ten Commandments.

JON: Okay Tom, why don't you read to us from Exodus 20:2, and tell us, **What is the preface to the Ten Commandments?**

TOM: **The preface to the Ten Commandments is in these words, I am the Lord thy God, which have brought thee out of the land of Egypt, out of the house of bondage.**

SARAH: In all my years as a Christian, I've never heard anyone talk about the significance of these introductory words in relation to the Ten Commandments. **What doth the preface to the Ten Commandments teach us?**

JON: **The preface to the Ten Commandments teacheth us, That because God is the Lord, and our God, and Redeemer, therefore we are bound to keep all his commandments.** In other words, we are bound to keep all of God's commandments for two reasons – first, because God is our Creator, and, second, because God is our Redeemer. Sarah, why don't you try explaining the first, while Tom does the second?

SARAH: Let me see – since the Creator has full authority over the creature, it is only right for the creature to obey his Maker perfectly in all things. Furthermore, man has been created in the image of God, and the only way that he is able to reflect and manifest God's moral image is by obeying His moral law. And when he does that, he brings glory to His Creator.

JON: Very good! How about you, Tom?

TOM: Well, the God who redeemed Israel out of Egypt also has redeemed each of us from the bondage and penalty of sin, and thus we ought to show our gratitude and love to Him by doing His will. The apostle John tells us that if we love God, we will keep His commandments (John 14:15). Also, God has redeemed fallen man for the very purpose of restoring him to His image and likeness. If we obey His commandments, we demonstrate that we are indeed God's redeemed people.

JON: You've both done well. Okay, let's stop at this point and continue next week.

Chapter 12

Man's Duty Towards God
(Part I, Q45-52)

F riday 7:30 p.m. (week 2)

THOMAS: Throughout this week, I've been thinking quite a bit about the sum of the Ten Commandments. The words, "Love God and love man" kept ringing in my ears. And the more I thought about it, the more I realised that it's not so easy to actually keep these commandments. I see at least two difficulties. First, we need to know what it really means to love God and to love man. After all, the natural man's concept of love is often quite different from what the Scriptures teach. Second, because of the fall, we are not at all inclined to obey God's commandments. It's against our sinful nature to do what's right in His sight.

JONATHAN: Well, as to your first difficulty, we will be looking at each commandment individually, and that should give us an idea of what it means to love God and to love man. As for your second, I must admit that it's a little more difficult to deal with. Although we have been made new creatures in Christ, there still remains in us this principle of sin, which we must struggle against till the end of our earthly journey. But because we've been renewed in the image of God, we now have the ability to choose between good or evil. We also have the Holy Spirit to enable us to keep His commandments. The more we grow in the grace of sanctification, the more we'll increase in our hatred for sin and in our love for God's law.

SARAH: How do you propose that we study each commandment?

JON: To answer that, I would like to ask another question: What does sin involve?

TOM: Sin involves not doing something you're supposed to do and doing something you're not supposed to do.

JON: Great. Now just as there are two parts to sin, there are also two parts to the law of God. In fact to be more accurate, I ought to say that because there are two sides to the law of God, there must necessarily be two sides to sin.

SARAH: I get it! Whenever we consider a commandment, we should ask, "What is required?" and "What is forbidden?"

JON: That's right. And as we proceed, you'll also notice that some of the commandments have special reasons attached to them.

TOM: **Which is the first commandment?**

JON: **The first commandment is, Thou shalt have no other gods before me.** This first commandment deals with the object of our worship. It tells us that we must have only one God, and this God must be the true and living God. This commandment thus rules out idolatry, or the worship of other gods, and atheism, or the denial of God's existence.

SARAH: **What is required in the first commandment?**

JON: **The first commandment requireth us to know and acknowledge God to be the only true God, and our God; and to worship and glorify him accordingly.** Before we can worship God, we must know the truth about Him as He is revealed to us in His Word. But besides knowing about Him, we also must know Him personally. He must be *our* God. Finally, we must worship and glorify Him accordingly. The measure of honour, glory, and love due a person depends on how honourable, glorious, and lovely that person is. Now our God is infinitely honourable, glorious, and lovely. It follows then that we owe Him all our praise, worship, and love. To give Him anything less is clearly unacceptable.

TOM: Looks like none of us can claim to have kept this commandment perfectly! All of us have rendered to God very much less than what He truly deserves and what we as creatures are able to render to Him. Could you give us some ways in which we may worship and glorify Him?

JON: We worship and glorify Him accordingly, by thinking, meditating, remembering, highly esteeming, honouring, adoring, choosing, loving, desiring, fearing of him; believing him; trusting, hoping, delighting, rejoicing in him; being zealous for him; calling upon him, giving all praise and thanks, and yielding all obedience and submission to him with the whole man; being careful in all things to please him, and sorrowful when in any thing he is offended; and walking humbly with him.[21]

SARAH: That's a real mouthful! I think we'll need to take some time to digest it. Meanwhile, **What is forbidden in the first commandment?**

JON: **The first commandment forbiddeth the denying, or not worshipping and glorifying the true God as God, and our God; and the giving of that worship and glory to any other, which is due to him alone.** Earlier I mentioned that the sins of idolatry and atheism are forbidden in this commandment. I should mention here that it is also a sin to have wrong and unworthy thoughts or opinions about God. We must search the Scriptures and believe everything that it teaches about God – adding nothing and subtracting nothing from it. Sarah, perhaps you could tell us, in the light of this first commandment, why discontentment in Christians is such a great sin.

SARAH: Well, a discontented Christian who murmurs against God about his lot in life is really saying one of two things: either God isn't sovereign and thus is unable to work all things out for the good of His people, or else

God isn't doing such a good job in taking care of His people and He could do better than that! Both of these are very unworthy thoughts of God and a definite breaking of the first commandment.

JON: That's right! Indeed, all of us need to guard ourselves against this sin because it's so easy to fall into it.

TOM: What does "before me" in the first commandment mean? **What are we especially taught by these words** *before me* **in the first commandment?**

JON: **These words** *before me* **in the first commandment teach us, That God, who seeth all things, taketh notice of, and is much displeased with, the sin of having any other God.**

SARAH: I like the first part of that statement! It's very comforting and assuring to know that God watches over us all the time and that He takes notice of every little detail. For example, when I'm in danger, He protects me. When I'm in distress, He comforts me. When I'm hurt, He comes to me with healing. Nothing is too small for Him to take notice of, and nothing is too big that He cannot deal with it.

JON: Yes, it's wonderful to know that God watches over us every moment and that He cares for us very much. But we mustn't forget the responsibilities that come with such a privilege. We need to be careful not to have any other gods in our lives. God will be very displeased with us if He finds us committing the sin of idolatry.

TOM: But is it possible for Christians to have other gods?

JON: Why not? Let me give you some examples. First, if we trust in anything more than God, we make it a god. If we trust in riches, we make riches a god. If we trust in our wisdom, we make wisdom a god. If we trust in ourselves, we make a god of ourselves! Second, if we love anything more than God, we make it a god. If we love our possessions, our pleasures, our friends, and even our own lives more than God, we make these things our gods. So you see, we have to be very careful, or we'll end up having many gods!

SARAH: **Which is the second commandment?**

JON: **The second commandment is, Thou shalt not make unto thee any graven image, or any likeness of any thing that is in heaven above, or that is in the earth beneath, or that is in the water under the earth. Thou shalt not bow down thyself to them, nor serve them: for I the Lord thy God am a jealous God, visiting the iniquity of the fathers upon the children unto the third and fourth generation of them that hate me; and showing mercy unto thousands of them that love me, and keep my commandments.**

TOM: It seems to me that the first commandment tells us *whom* we are to worship, while the second commandment tells us *how* we ought to worship Him.

JON: That's right. Sadly, though, there are many Christians today who break this commandment without

94

even realising it. We must understand that God is concerned about the way in which we worship Him. Just being sincere in our worship is not enough. Our sincerity must be accompanied by truth. Both of these are vital if we are to worship God in an acceptable manner. I think this is what Jesus meant when He said in John 4:24 that we must worship God in *spirit* and in *truth*.

SARAH: **What is required in the second commandment?**

JON: **The second commandment requireth the receiving, observing, and keeping pure and entire, all such religious worship and ordinances as God hath appointed in his Word.** The important principle in this commandment is the duty to worship God as He Himself commands. In other words, the Word of God ought to be our only rule to guide and direct us in worship. Everything we do in worship must be based on the Bible. On the other hand, anything without sound scriptural support is forbidden in worship. We must never worship God in any way that we like. That would be will-worship and unacceptable! Instead, we must receive, observe, and keep pure and complete everything about worship in God's Word -- nothing more and nothing less! The Lord, in Deuteronomy 12:30, warned the people not to follow after the pagan nations both in their object and in their manner of worship. And then He said in verse 32, "What thing soever I command you, observe to do it: thou shalt not add thereto, nor diminish from it."

TOM: Well, it looks like we really need to reconsider many of the things we do in worship each Lord's Day and ask ourselves if everything we're doing is indeed commanded by God. For a start, perhaps you could give us a list of things that ought to be done in worship.

JON: Prayer with thanksgiving, the reading of the Scriptures with godly fear, the sound preaching and conscionable hearing of the Word, in obedience unto God, with understanding, faith, and reverence; singing of psalms[22] with grace in the heart, and the proper administration and worthy receiving of the sacraments instituted by Christ.

SARAH: Your list seems to be pretty limited. How about worshipping God through the use of drama, choir, dancing, musical instruments, lighting of candles, waving of flags, pictures of Christ, and even the hymns and songs found in our church hymnbook? Aren't these things also acceptable in worship?

JON: Well, I'll be most willing to include any of these things (and any others) as long as you can prove to me from the Scriptures that these are indeed things God commands us to do and to use in New Testament worship! Remember that it's not enough just to show that the Scriptures do not forbid them; you'll need to show that there is positive scriptural warrant (either explicit commands or logical inferences) for something to be included as an element of worship.

SARAH: Okay, I'll think about it. Meanwhile, **What is forbidden in the second commandment?**

JON: **The second commandment forbiddeth the worshipping of God by images, or any other way not appointed in his Word.** I'd like to concentrate on the first part of this statement: "the worshipping of God by images." Some claim that the use of images helps a person to worship God better. This is clearly forbidden in the Word of God. Tom, can you think of some reasons why it is wrong to make an image of God?

TOM: God is a spirit, and no man has ever seen Him before. Surely you can't make an image of something you haven't seen before, much less create an image of God, who is an infinite and uncreated Spirit! Also, to set up an image to represent God is to debase Him. It is not right to represent the infinite God by that which is finite. Neither is it right to represent a living God with a lifeless object.

JON: Very good. We must worship God by faith and not by sight. God has given us His holy Word and His Holy Spirit to enable us to worship Him, and these are more than sufficient. Thomas Watson writes, "Is it not an absurd thing to bow down to the king's picture, when the king himself is present? It is more so to bow down to an image of God, when God himself is everywhere present."[23]

SARAH: Jon, I remember seeing many pictures and illustrations of Jesus during my years in junior Sunday school. Would you consider such pictures a violation of the second commandment?

JON: Well, we must realise that Christ is the second person of the Godhead. He is God Himself. To make an image or paint a picture of Christ for the purpose of worshipping Him through the image is indeed a violation of this commandment. Furthermore, no one actually knows what Jesus looked like while He was on earth. When an artist paints a picture of Jesus, he does so entirely out of his own imagination, and the result is not a true representation of Christ.

SARAH: But what if we don't worship Christ through these pictures? And don't you think that these pictures will help the little children to understand the Bible and the Gospel stories better?

JON: I don't think so. In fact, it is precisely because we want to teach the little children the truth that we shouldn't use such images. We want them to grow up understanding that God is a spirit and is without flesh and blood. And Christ, though He took to Himself human nature, did not cease to be God. He is no mere man but the God-man – worthy of all our worship and praise. We don't want them to grow up thinking that that was how Christ looked and, worse still, to have mental images of Christ when they worship Him, which would be mental idolatry. Let's honour God by teaching them in a God-honouring way.

TOM: I noticed that the second part of the second commandment gives us some reasons for keeping it, but what do they mean? **What are the reasons annexed to the second commandment?**

JON: **The reasons annexed to the second commandment are, God's sovereignty over us, his propriety in us, and the zeal he hath to his own worship.** There are basically three reasons given by God to motivate and encourage us to keep this commandment. First, our God is the Sovereign of the universe, and He alone determines how we should worship Him. Second, we belong to God and are His children. Just as children ought to love and obey their parents, so also should we love the Lord by doing what pleases Him. Third, our God is a jealous God, that is, He is very concerned that we worship Him in the right way, and He will surely punish all those who have little or no regard for His commandment.

Okay, it's been a rather long night of discussion. Let's end here.

Chapter 13

Man's Duty Towards God (Part II, Q53-62)

Friday 7:30 p.m. (week 3)

JONATHAN: We looked at the *object* (first commandment) and the *manner* (second commandment) of true worship last week. Today, we're going to consider the *attitude* (third commandment) and the *time* (fourth commandment) of worship. By the end of this session, we will have finished the first table of the law, that is, man's duty towards God. But I must first warn you that we'll probably end even later than last week!

THOMAS: Let's get started then! **Which is the third commandment?**

SARAH: **The third commandment is, Thou shalt not take the name of the Lord thy God in vain; for the Lord will not hold him guiltless that taketh his name in vain.** This commandment reminds me of something that Jesus Himself taught in the Lord's Prayer, which says, "Our Father which art in heaven, *Hallowed be thy name.*" It seems that the third commandment presents this truth in a negative way, while the Lord's Prayer puts it positively.

JON: Good observation. As we mentioned last week, each commandment has both a negative and a positive side to it. We are both required as well as forbidden to do certain things in each commandment. In this third commandment, we are taught what the right attitude in worship should be. It is not enough to worship the true God in a right manner but without a right attitude! I mentioned last week that sincerity without truth is unacceptable in worship. But truth without sincerity is equally abominable in the sight of God. In fact, this was the Lord's charge against some of the Pharisees and scribes. He said, "This people draweth nigh unto me with their mouth, and honoureth me with their lips; but their heart is far from me. But in vain they do worship me." (Matthew 15:8-9a). The word "vain" simply means careless and without meaning. To speak of God's name carelessly and without meaning is a sin, according to this commandment.

TOM: **What is required in the third commandment?**

JON: **The third commandment requireth the holy and reverent use of God's names, titles, attributes, ordinances, Word, and works.** Notice that the word "name" in the third commandment involves a lot more than what we would normally think of. The name of God tells us something about His nature, His attributes, and His works. In fact, the whole universe is a revelation of the meaning of God's name. Now, just by way of example, the name Beethoven is immediately associated with classical music, and it has meaning because of the many beautiful pieces of music he wrote, like his five piano concertos and especially his thirty-two piano sonatas and nine symphonies. Likewise God's name has meaning because of His great works of creation and providence. We don't really know God's name until we know who He is and what He has done. So we see that God's name is not an empty title but involves everything about Him.

SARAH: I guess we should be that much more careful and reverent when saying anything about God! I can think of at least three occasions during worship when it is possible to break this commandment. First, when we sing. It's so easy for us to get distracted by the melody or the singing that we don't focus on the words and consequently don't mean what we sing. Second, in prayer. When someone else is praying, our minds often wander when we are not watchful. In fact, I've even caught myself falling asleep during prayer on several occasions! Third, when the preacher is preaching. Needless to say, most of us are guilty of not listening carefully to what is being preached each week. Truly we take His name in vain if we sing or pray without meaning what we say. And we show Him great irreverence if we don't listen to Him speaking to us through His ministers.

JON: I recently read an interesting illustration about not paying attention during service. It goes like this: "All the members were seated in a church building for a Sunday morning worship service, and the minister had just begun his sermon when the interruptions started. First, Sally started playing with her pet kitten, Puff. Then George ran and jumped to catch a baseball. Patricia was soon pedaling her new bike at quite a speed and was just a flash as she went by. Mr Rodgers started cutting the wood he needed for the garage he was building. What a noise his sawing made! Mrs. Smith started cutting out her new dress, as Sandra saddled her horse and rode off at a full gallop. Jack gradually began working on his car engine. What distractions! At times, the voice of the minister could not even be heard. This certainly was a strange church service, don't you think? Sadly, the church service just described is not that strange. All these things took place without an actual sound in the church building … for they all happened in the minds of the 'listeners.' However, these poor 'listeners' never heard most of the sermon."[24]

TOM: Thanks for that illustration! It reminds me that it's possible to be physically present but mentally absent from worship. **What is forbidden in the third commandment?**

JON: **The third commandment forbiddeth all profaning and abusing of any thing whereby God maketh himself known.** It's a terrible thing to hear people use God's name as a common curse word in their conversations. We often hear such profanities in the movies and in television shows. As Christians, we should avoid watching such shows because we don't want to partake in the sins of these people. In fact, every time we hear God's name being taken in vain, we should feel a sense of godly anger and sorrow in our hearts because God is not glorified. We should learn from the psalmist, who said, "Rivers of waters run down mine eyes, because they keep not thy law" (Psalm 119:136).

TOM: It's possible to violate this commandment in our thoughts and words. But how about in our actions and deeds?

JON: Why not? For example, if we call ourselves Christians and don't behave as Christians, we take God's name in vain. As Christians, we are God's representatives in this world and ambassadors for Christ (2 Corinthians 5:20). If we live unholy lives and perform unrighteous deeds, we indeed profane and abuse the name of God.

SARAH: No wonder Jesus issued that stern warning in Matthew 7:21: "Not every one that saith unto me, Lord, Lord, shall enter into the kingdom of heaven." It's clear that these hypocrites, who professed to know Christ, were guilty of taking His name in vain, because they weren't His true disciples in the first place; and, consequently, He was never really their Lord.

TOM: **What is the reason annexed to the third commandment?**

JON: **The reason annexed to the third commandment is, That however the breakers of this commandment may escape punishment from men, yet the Lord our God will not suffer (allow) them to escape his righteous judgment.** By now, you have noticed that it's possible to break this commandment without anyone else knowing about it. After all, no one has access to our thoughts and inward attitudes in worship except God. And God, who alone is the righteous Judge, will not allow anyone who breaks this commandment (or any other commandment for that matter) to escape. Always remember that!

SARAH: **Which is the fourth commandment?**

TOM: **The fourth commandment is, Remember the Sabbath day, to keep it holy. Six days shalt thou labour, and do all thy work; but the seventh day is the Sabbath of the Lord thy God: in it thou shalt not do any work, thou, nor thy son, nor thy daughter, thy man-servant, nor thy maid-servant, nor thy cattle, nor thy stranger that is within thy gates: for in six days the Lord made heaven and earth, the sea, and all that in them is, and rested the seventh day: wherefore the Lord blessed the Sabbath day, and hallowed it.** Based on what I've observed, it seems that many Christians today don't take this commandment very seriously. Most would say that it's only for the Jews and not for others and that it's part of the ceremonial rather than moral law. On the other hand, there are those who insist that we must keep the Sabbath in a very strict and legalistic way. For example, we must refrain from walking a certain distance, from cooking, and from washing on the Sabbath day. What then should our attitude towards the fourth commandment be?[25]

JON: I must say that both these extremes are wrong. The fourth commandment is indeed a moral law, and if it is a moral law, it is universally (for everyone) and perpetually (in all ages) binding. Let me briefly give three reasons why this is so. First, the Sabbath was a Creation ordinance. In other words, at Creation (even before the fall of man) God instructed man to observe the Sabbath. Genesis 2:3 says, "And God blessed the seventh day, and sanctified it: because that in it he had rested from all his work which God created and made." Some people claim that the Sabbath commandment was only given at Mount Sinai and not before that. Yet the commandment itself claims a Creation origin when it says, "In six days the Lord made heaven and earth...and rested on the seventh day" (Exodus 20:11). Second, God wrote all ten commandments with His own finger on two tables of stone. All the other laws and commandments were written by Moses. This strongly indicates to us that the Ten Commandments are special and distinct from the other laws and commandments. They belong to a class by themselves! Now, very few Christians would say that the other nine commandments are not moral. Yet how can any of them say that the fourth commandment is not moral when it is written among nine others that are? It would require very strong evidence to prove that this commandment isn't part of the moral law. Third, this commandment is consistent with the New Testament. In fact, there isn't a place in the New Testament that teaches us the abrogation of this commandment. When Christ apparently "violated" the Sabbath day, He didn't actually break the commandment of God. Instead, what He broke was the traditions and rules set by man. Furthermore, if Christ had indeed broken the fourth commandment, the Jews would have used it against Him in His trial! Christ came to fulfill the law, not to break it. By His perfect obedience, He satisfied divine justice for us and earned for us the reward of eternal life. And Christ has saved us so that we too will keep the moral law and thus glorify God.

SARAH: I can't say that I'm fully convinced of the applicability of the Sabbath commandment for the New Testament Christian, but I must say that your arguments are fairly persuasive. But let's carry on our discussion on this topic. **What is required in the fourth commandment?**

JON: **The fourth commandment requireth the keeping holy to God such set times as he hath appointed in his Word; expressly one whole day in seven, to be a holy Sabbath to himself.** At creation God blessed and sanctified the seventh day. To sanctify something is to set apart or separate it from the rest. Likewise, God requires all of us to set aside one whole day each week for Him. This day is to be a very special one unlike all others. You see, the Sabbath is both a relic of Paradise and an emblem and type of heaven. In other words, it reminds us of the perfect and wonderful state of man in the garden before the fall (incidentally, even in Paradise, man needed a Sabbath!), and it also helps us look forward to our eternal home in heaven, where we shall enjoy a never-ending Sabbath in the presence of God!

TOM: If I'm not wrong, the Jews begin their Sabbath observance on a Friday evening, and it lasts all the way till Saturday evening. But Christians observe the Christian Sabbath, or the Lord's Day, on a Sunday. **Which day of the seven hath God appointed to be the weekly Sabbath?**

JON: **From the beginning of the world to the resurrection of Christ, God appointed the seventh day of the week to be the weekly Sabbath; and the first day of the week ever since, to continue to the end of the world, which is the Christian Sabbath.** Notice that God didn't appoint Saturday to be the Sabbath, but rather He appointed the seventh day. The commandment itself doesn't tell us that we must keep the Sabbath on the last day of the week. It only tells us that we must keep one day out of every seven. It is the proportion of time and not the order of days that is fixed by this commandment. At creation, God rested after six days of creative work, and so the last day of the week became the Sabbath. But God later changed the Sabbath to the first day of the week when He raised up the Lord Jesus Christ on that day (Psalm 118:22-24).

SARAH: **How is the Sabbath to be sanctified?**

JON: **The Sabbath is to be sanctified by a holy resting all that day, even from such worldly employments and recreations as are lawful on other days; and spending the whole time in the public and private exercises of God's worship, except so much as is to be taken up in the works of necessity and mercy.**

TOM: I always had the wrong impression that Sabbath keeping simply meant doing nothing the whole day, apart from going to church for a few hours. I didn't realise that Sabbath keeping is not just about putting aside our secular work and recreation but also involves actively worshipping and seeking God both publicly and privately.

JON: Yes, that's right. But I would remind us that while we are to keep the Sabbath day holy unto the Lord, we are not to live in any way we please on the other six days. There is a sense in which each day should be holy unto the Lord. But it is on the Lord's Day that we are able to spend the entire day worshipping Him without having to concentrate on our worldly business. The only exception to this is when there are works of mercy and necessity that require our attention. Works of mercy include looking after a sick person or even lifting a helpless animal out of a pit. Works of necessity are things that cannot be done on another day or things necessary for the proper preservation and sustenance of life.

SARAH: How do we spend the whole day in public and private exercises of worship?

JON: May I suggest, first, that we should start preparing for the Sabbath the night before by breaking off from our work as early as we can, getting our hearts and minds ready for worship, and having a good night's rest. Second, we should arise early in the morning to spend time in meditation of the works of God in Creation and redemption and in the reading of God's Word and other suitable Christian books that will help us to focus our thoughts upon Him.[26] We should pray for God's presence to be with us throughout the day, that He will speak to us through His ministers, and that we would be enabled to worship Him from a sincere heart without distraction. Third, after coming back from church, we should spend time, either individually or, if possible, as a family, repeating to ourselves and meditating upon all that we have learned in church so that these lessons will take root in our lives and bring forth fruits. Finally, we should close the day in secret prayer once again, thanking God for all His mercies, humbly confessing our sins, and asking for further supplies of grace for the week ahead. The Puritan Thomas Vincent, writing about the Lord's Day says, "When the day is at an end, we should long for the Sabbath in heaven, which will never have an end."[27] These are just some suggestions for spending the Lord's Day in a meaningful manner. Remember that we should learn to call the Sabbath a delight and to enjoy the whole day in God's presence (Isaiah 58:13).

TOM: **What is forbidden in the fourth commandment?**

JON: **The fourth commandment forbiddeth the omission or careless performance of the duties required, and the profaning the day by idleness, or doing that which is in itself sinful, or by unnecessary thoughts, words, or works, about our worldly employments or recreations.** As much as possible, we should avoid doing those things that distract us from focusing our attention upon God. Any unnecessary thoughts, words, and actions should be excluded. Also, the Lord's Day should not be used as an excuse for idleness. There is something about this fourth commandment that is often overlooked. In the commandment, God says, "Six days shalt thou labour, and do all thy work." Not only are we to keep the Sabbath holy, but we are also to work hard throughout the rest of the week. God commands us to do the work He has given us to the best of our ability. We are not to be lazy or idle in our vocation. When we do our work faithfully, we glorify God. If we don't, we break His commandment and dishonour Him.

SARAH: **What are the reasons annexed to the fourth commandment?**

JON: **The reasons annexed to the fourth commandment are, God's allowing us six days of the week for our own employments, his challenging a special propriety in the seventh, his own example, and his blessing the Sabbath day.** Ultimately, this commandment is for the glory of God and for the good of His people. I love the words of the Lord in the book of Malachi, when He said, "Will a man rob God? Yet ye have robbed me. ... Bring ye all the tithes into the storehouse, that there may be meat in mine house, and prove me now herewith, saith the LORD of hosts, if I will not open you the windows of heaven, and pour you out a blessing, that there shall not be room enough to receive it" (Malachi 3:8, 10). I really believe that if Christians today would take the fourth commandment seriously, God would shower upon us and upon His church such a blessing that there would not be room enough to receive it!

Chapter 14

Man's Duty Towards Man (Part I, Q63-72)

Friday 7:30 p.m. (week 4)

JONATHAN: We finished the first table of the law last week after a very long session! For this evening, we'll look at the first half of the second table, that is, the fifth to the seventh commandments. As we proceed, let's remember that the second table of the law has to do primarily with loving our neighbours as ourselves.

THOMAS: **Which is the fifth commandment?**

SARAH: **The fifth commandment is, Honour thy father and thy mother; that thy days may be long upon the land which the Lord thy God giveth thee.** I would like to start by asking, "Who are meant by father and mother in this commandment?"

JON: For many years, I used to think that "father and

mother" simply referred to my earthly parents and no one else. Later on, I started to ask, What about my grandparents? Shouldn't I also honour them? How about my aunts and uncles? And how about my principal and my teachers at school and all those in authority over me? How about my church leaders and my pastor? Finally, how about my peers and even those below me? Shouldn't I honour all these people too? Slowly, I realised that this commandment had to involve a lot more people than just my own earthly parents. Romans 13:1 says, "Let every soul be subject unto the higher powers. For there is no power but of God: the powers that be are ordained of God."

TOM: **What is required in the fifth commandment?**

JON: **The fifth commandment requireth the preserving the honour, and performing the duties, belonging to every one in their several places and relations, as superiors, inferiors, or equals.** Note that the phrase "superior, inferiors, or equals" doesn't just refer to age but also includes all sorts of relationships. After all, it's possible to have a superior at work who is younger than you are, isn't it?

TOM: How do we preserve the honour and perform the duties towards our superiors?

JON: We must show them due reverence in heart, word, and behaviour; pray and give thanks for them; be willing to obey their lawful commands and counsels; submit to their correction; and bear with their weaknesses and infirmities by covering them in love.

SARAH: How about our inferiors?

JON: Well, according to the authority we've been given and our relationship with them, we should love, pray for, instruct, encourage, admonish, and counsel them. Also, we should protect and provide for them and be a good example to them in speech and conduct.

SARAH: **What is forbidden in the fifth commandment?**

JON: **The fifth commandment forbiddeth the neglecting of, or doing any thing against, the honour and duty which belongeth to every one in their several places and relations.**

TOM: What are some of the ways in which we can sin against our superiors?

JON: We sin against our superiors by neglecting the duties we owe them, envying, rebelling against, showing contempt of, cursing, mocking and disobeying them.

SARAH: And our inferiors?

JON: Besides neglecting the duties required of us, we sin by seeking our own profit, ease, and pleasure without due consideration for them; commanding them to do things unlawful; encouraging and counseling them to do evil; discouraging and dissuading them from doing good; exposing them to temptation and danger; correcting them unnecessarily; and provoking them to anger.

TOM: **What is the reason annexed to the fifth commandment?**

JON: **The reason annexed to the fifth commandment, is a promise of long life and prosperity (as far as it shall serve for God's glory and their own good) to all such as keep this commandment.** This is the first commandment with a specific promise attached (Ephesians 6:2). Now the blessing that God promises us is a long and blessed life upon this earth, so long as it shall be to God's glory and our good. This is to be understood as being a general rather than a universal rule. In other words, there will be exceptions to this rule, but for the most part, those who obey this commandment will receive the promise attached to it.

SARAH: **Which is the sixth commandment?**

JON: **The sixth commandment is, Thou shalt not kill.** The important principle behind this commandment is that murder, or the unjust killing of a human person, is wrong because man is made in the image of God. God is the giver of all life, and no one has the right to take it away without a just cause. And remember, that includes our own lives too!

TOM: **What is required in the sixth commandment?**

JON: **The sixth commandment requireth all lawful endeavours to preserve our own life, and the life of others.** In this commandment, we are instructed to do what we can to preserve our lives and the lives of others.

For example, it would be wrong to leave someone to die when you clearly have the power to prevent it. Also, it would be wrong not to warn someone of a danger that you are aware of. And it is foolish to do anything that may endanger your own life or the lives of other people.

SARAH: I was wondering if this commandment applies to the soul just as it does to the body. After all, didn't Jesus imply that our life is more than just the body when He said, "Fear not them which kill the body…but rather fear him which is able to destroy both soul and body in hell" (Matthew 10:28)?

JON: Good point. Yes, we should never injure the soul of another person either, and it's possible to do that by setting a bad example for others to follow, by enticing others to sin, and by influencing others away from good. But ultimately the best way to keep this commandment is to do all we can to seek eternal life for those who are on their way to hell. If you saw a person trapped in a burning house, surely you would try your very best to rescue him before he burns to death. Yet, we sometimes forget that all people without Christ are in danger of burning in hell forever!

SARAH: Thanks for that reminder. **What is forbidden in the sixth commandment?**

JON: **The sixth commandment forbiddeth the taking away of our own life, or the life of our neighbour unjustly, or whatsoever tendeth thereunto.** I once heard a story that illustrates this commandment very well.

It goes something like this: "A mother who was carrying her one-year old child in her arms went to a doctor's office to ask for an abortion. 'Doctor,' she said, 'I need your help. I am expecting a child again and I cannot take care of two children so close in age.' 'If you want one of the children to be killed,' answered the doctor calmly, picking up a sharp knife, 'why don't we kill the one in your arms? That will be much easier and safer for you.' Seeing the doctor approach her child with a knife in his hand, the woman almost fainted. Then, jumping up, she screamed, 'Murderer!' The doctor then calmed her down and explained that by asking for an abortion, she had just asked him to murder the child growing inside her, and that he could no more murder the unborn child than the one in her arms."[28] Indeed, abortion is an example of the unjust taking of life.

SARAH: It is terrible to think that millions of unborn babies around the world each year are murdered in the womb!

JON: Yes, it's terrible indeed, and that is what happens when people abandon the law of God. As an aside, I should mention that God's Word does not forbid every kind of killing of persons. For example, it is not wrong for the law courts to pass the death sentence upon certain criminals worthy of capital punishment. And neither is it wrong to kill in self-defense or in war.

TOM: Jesus mentioned in His Sermon on the Mount that it is wrong to be angry with another person without a just cause (Matthew 5:22). Does that mean that even the slightest evil thought about someone is a violation of this commandment?

JON: Yes, it is. And it's even worse if we allow these evil thoughts, such as sinful anger, hatred, envy, and desire for revenge, to continually remain in our minds. The moment such thoughts come to our mind, we should immediately repent and seek the Lord's pardon. Remember, if we allow evil thoughts to fester, sooner or later, they will result in evil actions. The Puritan Richard Baxter once said, "A lustful thought is from the same defiled puddle as actual filthiness: and the thought is but the passage to the action: it is but the same sin in its minority, tending to maturity."[29]

SARAH: **Which is the seventh commandment?**

JON: **The seventh commandment is, Thou shalt not commit adultery.** Remember that our God is a faithful and covenant-keeping God, who never breaks His covenants. Thus to commit adultery is to insult and disregard the faithfulness of God, and that is a great sin against Him. If we are to accurately reflect the image of God, especially His faithfulness, we must keep this commandment.

TOM: **What is required in the seventh commandment?**

JON: **The seventh commandment requireth the preservation of our own and our neighbour's chastity, in heart, speech, and behaviour.** This commandment has to do with keeping our lives pure and free from all lustful thoughts, words, and deeds. We must understand that our body is not our own but is the temple of the Holy Spirit. Paul says in 1 Corinthians 6:19-20, "What? know ye not that your body is the temple of the Holy Ghost which is in you, which ye have of God, and ye are not your own? For ye are bought with a price: therefore glorify God in your body, and in your spirit, which are God's."

SARAH: What are some practical ways we can preserve our own and our neighbour's chastity?

JON: First, we should set a watch over our eyes and our senses, and be careful not to allow any unclean thing to enter in. Avoid the places or the things that will most likely tempt you to sin. Watch what you read in books and magazines and what you see on the television and the Internet. Keep away from all appearances of evil. Second, never allow yourself to remain idle for any period of time. Someone once said that when we are idle, we tempt the devil to tempt us! When King David was idling on his rooftop, he saw Bathsheba bathing and later committed adultery with her. Let us rather be well employed in the Lord's vineyard so that when the devil comes, we will have no time to listen to his temptation. Third, we should labour to get the fear of God in our hearts. When Joseph was tempted by Potiphar's wife, he said, "How … can I do this great wickedness, and sin against God?" (Genesis 39:9). We should fear God, not only because He punishes all iniquity, but also because we are afraid of offending a God as gracious and loving as He.

TOM: **What is forbidden in the seventh commandment?**

JON: **The seventh commandment forbiddeth all unchaste thoughts, words, and actions.** If we truly love someone, we will not have any impure thoughts about that person. And neither will we do or say anything to cause that person to sin.

Chapter 15

Man's Duty Towards Man (Part II, Q73-81)

F riday 7:30 p.m. (week 5)

JONATHAN: We've finally arrived at our last session on the Ten Commandments; and by the end of the meeting, we will have covered the second table of the law, namely our duty towards our fellow man. This evening, we're going to look at two commandments that have stirred up some controversy among Christians and one commandment that has to do primarily with our inward attitude.

THOMAS: That should be interesting. **Which is the eighth commandment?**

SARAH: **The eighth commandment is, Thou shalt not steal.** But what does it really mean to "steal"?

JON: To answer that, we need to ask, "What are the legitimate ways in which we may obtain something?" Stealing would then be defined as the acquiring of anything apart from these legitimate means. I can think of just two lawful means of getting anything. Do you know what they are?

TOM: By working for it or by receiving it as a gift.

JON: That's right. Keep that in mind as we move on.

SARAH: **What is required in the eighth commandment?**

TOM: **The eighth commandment requireth the lawful procuring and furthering the wealth and outward estate of ourselves and others.**

SARAH: **What is forbidden in the eighth commandment?**

TOM: **The eighth commandment forbiddeth whatsoever doth or may unjustly hinder our own or our neighbour's wealth or outward estate.**

JON: Tom has already mentioned the two means of lawful procurement. Sarah, can you give us an example of unlawful procurement?

SARAH: It is openly or secretly taking something that doesn't belong to you. This would include robbery, theft, and even fraud. It is wrong to cheat someone or mislead him into giving you more than what he should. A good example of this would be in the use of deceptive advertisements that mislead people into buying something they don't need or into thinking that they are getting more than what they are really getting.

JON: Another form of stealing would be gambling. In gambling, a person tries to obtain wealth without labouring for it or receiving it as gift. Although in many countries gambling is legal, in God's sight, it's not acceptable. In this commandment, we are called to a faithful use of all the resources God puts in our charge. We must always acknowledge that God is the ultimate owner of everything in this universe. And He graciously gives us many things in this life to use and to enjoy. We are responsible to put these things to good and profitable use. Remember that we must always glorify God by the way we use our resources. Thus it would be wrong to waste or to spend unnecessarily on things. On the other hand, it also would be wrong to withhold from giving to others (or ourselves) what is rightfully due. For example, to be slothful or idle while at work is wrong because that would be robbing your employer of the time that he is paying you to do your job.

TOM: Talking about time robbery, how about showing up late for an appointment? Is that also a breaking of this commandment?

JON: Yes, it is a sin to steal time from others by making them wait for us unnecessarily when it is within our power to arrive on time.

SARAH: And how about buying or using imitation goods like pirated software?

JON: Yes, I believe we should avoid the use of such items because they unjustly hinder our neighbour's wealth or outward estate. Indeed, there are many other ways in which this commandment may be violated. There are also many occasions in which we may be tempted to compromise our standards with regard to this commandment. We must be watchful at all times and pray for wisdom to discern what is and what isn't a breaking of this commandment. Finally, let's remember that our God is a God of justice. To break this eighth commandment is to sin against the justice of God.

TOM: **Which is the ninth commandment?**

JON: **The ninth commandment is, Thou shalt not bear false witness against thy neighbour.** Truth is one of the attributes of God, and it is not difficult to see why God requires His people to be truthful as well. Satan, on the other hand, is called the father of lies (John 8:44). If we walk in truth, we will resemble our heavenly Father and manifest ourselves as His true children. If not, we will resemble the devil and demonstrate that we are in all probability the devil's children!

SARAH: **What is required in the ninth commandment?**

JON: **The ninth commandment requireth the maintaining and promoting of truth between man and man, and of our own and our neighbour's good**

name, especially in witness-bearing. There are two things required in this commandment: first, to promote truth between fellow men; and, second, to promote our own good name and that of our neighbour. In other words, not only are we to speak the truth when talking to our neighbour, but we are also to speak the truth when talking to other people about our neighbour. This commandment excludes all methods of falsifying the truth and also of slandering another person.

SARAH: Are there any exceptions to speaking the truth? Or to put it in another way, do certain circumstances justify a lie?

JON: Here is where the controversy surrounding this commandment lies. I'll give three instances where some have claimed that it is justifiable to lie, and we'll examine each one. First is lying to make someone feel good -- for example, telling someone who can't sing that he sings beautifully. Second is lying to prevent an unpleasant situation or an inconvenience from occurring -- for example, refusing to take a telephone call from someone you don't want to talk to by asking a colleague to lie to that person, saying that you're not available. Third is lying in order to save your own life or the lives of other people -- for example Rahab's lie to protect the spies (Joshua 2). Tom, what do you think of these three instances?

TOM: The first situation is a case of flattery. Although it may not necessarily be harmful to any one, I believe it is still wrong to do it. Psalm 12:3 says, "The LORD shall cut off all flattering lips." The second instance is still very much a lie, and certainly the end cannot justify the means. As Christians, no matter how unpleasant or inconvenient the situation may be, we should speak the truth and trust that the Lord will work things well for His people. In fact, it is a double sin to lie with someone else's help, as in the example you gave. As for the third instance, I can't say for sure, but it does seem to me that it is not wrong to lie in such situations and that what Rahab did was actually right. After all, if she had told the king's men that the spies were indeed hiding in her house, she would have betrayed them as well as betrayed their trust in her, and that would not be right.

JON: This is a difficult question, and there are various views on it. Personally, I'm inclined to agree with you that Rahab did no wrong in the way she protected the spies and that under certain extreme circumstances when someone's life is unjustly threatened, particularly in times of war, it is not wrong to deceive the enemy. But having said that, I also must say that we must never use Rahab's example to justify any kind of deception. Instead, we should study very carefully the situations in Scripture in which deception in permitted and then look for parallel situations in our own lives in order to decide whether or not it is right to deceive.

TOM: **What is forbidden in the ninth commandment?**

JON: **The ninth commandment forbiddeth whatsoever is prejudicial to truth, or injurious to our own or our neighbour's good name.** I mentioned that it is sometimes wise to conceal or withhold the truth. But that is not always the right thing to do either. In fact, it would be wrong to conceal the truth when doing so would result in someone getting hurt or in a wrong being done. Sinful silence can be as bad as speaking falsehood. Again, we need wisdom from God to know what to say and what not to say. Indeed, before saying anything, it's always good to ask, "Would Jesus have me say this?" and "Will God be pleased if I said that?" Ultimately, it is God whom we want to please and not man.

SARAH: That's a helpful suggestion. Okay, one more: **Which is the tenth commandment?**

JON: **The tenth commandment is, Thou shalt not covet thy neighbour's house, thou shalt not covet thy neighbour's wife, nor his man-servant, nor his maid-servant, nor his ox, nor his ass, nor any thing that is thy neighbour's.** As I mentioned earlier, this commandment has to do primarily with our inward attitude. Although it is true that the violation of it may manifest itself in other outward sins, most of the time this sin is committed inside our hearts and only we ourselves know about it.

TOM: **What is required in the tenth commandment?**

JON: **The tenth commandment requireth full contentment with our own condition, with a right and charitable frame of spirit toward our neighbour, and all that is his.** The two things required in this commandment are, first, contentment with our own condition, and, second, a right and charitable attitude toward our neighbour's condition. Both these things are closely related. If we are contented with our own condition, we will not covet our neighbour's possessions. On the other hand, if we are dissatisfied with what we have, there will be a great tendency for us to look at things that don't belong to us in an envious and lustful manner.

SARAH: I like what the apostle Paul said in Philippians 4:11: "Not that I speak in respect of want: for I have learned, in whatsoever state I am, therewith to be content." Again he said in 1 Thessalonians 5:16 and 18, "Rejoice evermore. … In every thing give thanks: for this is the will of God in Christ Jesus concerning you." If Paul could find contentment even in great trials and sufferings, surely we ought to be contented with our present condition.

JON: That's right. In fact, very often, we are guilty of the same sin as the Israelites as they wandered in the wilderness. They were often dissatisfied with what they had and lusted after the things they did not have.

TOM: **What is forbidden in the tenth commandment?**

JON: **The tenth commandment forbiddeth all discontentment with our own estate, envying or grieving at the good of our neighbour, and all inordinate motions and affections to any thing that is his.** Do we complain and murmur against God for what He has given or withheld from us in life? Are we grieved at the advancement and success of our neighbour, and do we have evil and envious thoughts about him? If so, we have transgressed this commandment. And remember that the sin of covetousness is equated with the sin of idolatry (Ephesians 5:5).

SARAH: What are the signs of a covetous spirit?

JON: First, if one has a covetous spirit, his thoughts are wholly taken up by the things of the world. Instead of thinking about Christ and of heaven, he thinks about profit, pleasure, and honour. Second, his words and conversations are all about this world. He speaks little of eternal things but much of those things that are temporal. Third, he labours diligently after the world, as if this world were his eternal home, and neglects the well-being of his soul. In fact, he may even be willing to exchange heaven and eternal life for the treasures that this world has to offer. Many people today, including Christians, have been eaten up by such a spirit of covetousness. Let's be careful.

TOM: Allow me to illustrate a covetous spirit from my own experience.[30] When I was five years old, I had a tricycle, but I didn't like it anymore. I wanted a two-wheeler. "If I had a two-wheeler bike, I'd be happy," I told myself. After I received a two-wheeler bike, I seemed happy for a few weeks, but then I started wishing for a ten-speed mountain bike. "If only I had a ten-speed like Jeff's," I kept thinking, "then I'd be happy." Later, I received a new ten-speed mountain bike, and I was happy for a time. But soon I started wishing for a motorcycle. "If only I had a motorcycle," I thought. Then some years later, a few months after I got a motorcycle, I thought, "Boy, if I only had a neat car like Bob's. Wouldn't that be something?" And on and on it went. Indeed, we need to watch out for covetousness at all stages and in all areas of our life.

Chapter 16

The Law of God and Sin (Q82-84)

Friday 7:30 p.m. (week 6)

JONATHAN: I'm not sure about the both of you, but I've personally enjoyed our past five sessions on the law of God. I'm sure there's a lot more we can learn about the moral law. For a start, allow me to recommend A. W. Pink's book on the Ten Commandments.[31] I found it pretty easy to read and very helpful. It's important that we constantly review all the Ten Commandments and examine our lives in the light of each one of them. Always remember that knowing the commandments and actually keeping them are both essential if we are to glorify God.

THOMAS: I fully agree with you. It's easy to go away from a Bible study or a worship service feeling joyful and excited about what we've learned but forgetting that hearing and learning is only part of our duty. We're required to apply these truths in our lives. James 1:22 says,

"But be ye doers of the word, and not hearers only, deceiving your own selves."

JON: What about you, Sarah? Any thoughts on what we've discussed so far?

SARAH: Well, I've learned that as God's people, we should love to keep His law because we love Him. I'm slowly beginning to understand the apostle John's statement in 1 John 5:3, "His commandments are not grievous." And I've been praying, "Teach me, O Lord, the way of thy statutes; and I shall keep it unto the end. Give me understanding, and I shall keep thy law; yea I shall observe it with my whole heart" (Psalm 119:33-34).

TOM: It's sad that many Christians today find God's law grievous and troublesome. What a far cry from the psalmist, who said, "Oh how love I thy law! it is my meditation all the day" (Psalm 119:97).

JON: I'm glad to hear that we've all learned some things over the past few weeks. Now that we've looked at the moral law of God and its requirements, a logical question to ask is whether any man is able to keep God's commandments perfectly. **Is any man able perfectly to keep the commandments of God?**

SARAH: I'd like to try to answer that: **No mere man since the Fall is able in this life perfectly to keep the commandments of God, but doth daily break them in thought, word, and deed.**

JON: Very good! Tom, perhaps you'd like to comment on Sarah's answer.

TOM: I have two observations to make. First, no mere man (and that excludes Christ, because He is no mere man but the God-man) has or will ever be able to keep God's law perfectly while he's still living on this earth. Even Adam, who for a short period of time enjoyed perfect sinlessness, fell from that state of perfection by sinning against God; and from that time onward, he lived out the rest of his life on earth as a sinner, just like all his descendents.

SARAH: Pardon me for interrupting, but I was just wondering if it's possible for a Christian to attain perfection in this life.

JON: Interesting question. There are some Christians who believe and teach what theologians call perfectionism. Before I answer that question, I want to remind us that keeping God's law perfectly involves keeping *all* the commandments of God at *all* times without the slightest breach of any of them in terms of our inclination, disposition, thought, word, or deed. In other words, our entire being, both body and soul, must be in perfect conformity to God's law constantly.

TOM: That's a tall order. I'm fairly certain that no one can achieve that in this life!

JON: You're right. Besides our own daily experience, which testifies to what you've said, the Bible shows us very clearly that no one will ever attain perfection in this life. First, it records for us the sins of the most holy saints who ever lived, including David, Moses, Job, Noah, Abraham, and others. If such great saints could still sin, it is unlikely that any saint can be totally without sin in this life. Second, the Bible teaches us explicitly, in a number of passages, that no one, not even a Christian, is without sin. Some examples are 1 John 1:8 and 10: "If we say that we have no sin, we deceive ourselves, and the truth is not in us. ... If we say that we have not sinned, we make him a liar, and his word is not in us"; 1 Kings 8:46: "For there is no man that sinneth not"; and Ecclesiastes 7:20: "For there is not a just man upon earth, that doeth good, and sinneth not." Third, the apostle Paul wrote in Romans 7 concerning the principle of sin that still remains in us and the struggles that we'll face in this life. He also wrote in Galatians 5:17, "For the flesh lusteth against the Spirit, and the Spirit against the flesh; and these are contrary the one to the other: so that ye cannot do the things that ye would." Now even though we won't be perfect in this life, we must still strive against sin and strive to lead holy lives. Those who refuse to do so and who think that they will still go to heaven will be badly mistaken. Hebrews 12:14 states, "Follow peace with all men, and holiness, without which no man shall see the Lord."

SARAH: I guess we'll have to wait patiently till we reach heaven before we attain perfection!

JON: Someone once said, "Perfection is the aim of this life, but it is the reward of another life. We should endeavor after perfection in grace, but we shall not attain it till grace is perfected in glory." Well, that's another reason to look forward to our heavenly home! Tom, earlier you mentioned that you had another observation to make about Sarah's answer.

TOM: Well, I observed that there are basically just three areas of our lives in which we may sin against God: in our thoughts, words, and deeds.

JON: Yes, and we must constantly watch out for each of them. Remember also that it is not enough just to abstain from sins of commission; we also must take heed of sins of omission too! An example of such a sin is found in 1 Samuel 12:23. Samuel said to the people, "Moreover as for me, God forbid that I should sin against the Lord in ceasing to pray for you." To Samuel, failure to pray for the people was considered a sin.

TOM: I've been thinking recently about whether all sins are equally evil or whether some are worse than others. **Are all transgressions of the law equally heinous?**

JON: **Some sins, in themselves, and by reason of several aggravations, are more heinous in the sight of God than others.**

SARAH: That's new! I never knew that there were degrees of sin. I've always been taught that any sin is just as sinful as every other sin because every sin by itself deserves a hell all of its own.

JON: It's true that every sin deserves eternal punishment, but notice that even in hell, there will be degrees of punishment corresponding to the quality and quantity of sins committed! Let me give you a few scriptural proofs for this doctrine. First, in John 19:11 Jesus said to Pilate, "Therefore he that delivered me unto thee hath the **greater** sin." Christ was speaking about Caiaphas the high priest, who had just delivered Him over to Pilate for execution. The very fact that Caiaphas was charged with a greater sin shows us that there must be degrees of sin. Second, in Ezekiel 8:6 we find these words: "But turn thee yet again, and thou shalt see **greater** abominations." In this verse, Ezekiel was given a vision of the wicked things done by the children of Israel in the temple. As the chapter proceeds, God reveals to Ezekiel increasing degrees of abomination. Notice again the word "greater." Third, I'm sure you're familiar with the unpardonable sin, which Jesus spoke of in Matthew 12:31-32. Now if there is one sin that God will not pardon, it clearly indicates to us that there is a difference in degree between that particular sin and all other sins. Fourth, we read in Matthew 11:22: "But I say unto you, It shall be more tolerable for Tyre and Sidon at the day of judgment, than for you." In this passage, Jesus rebuked those cities in which He had done many of His mighty works, because they did not repent. The words "more tolerable" suggest that there are degrees of punishment due to the different degrees of sin. Finally, in Luke 12:47-48, Jesus says, "And that servant, which knew his lord's will, and prepared not himself, neither did according to his will, shall be beaten with many stripes. But he that knew not, and did commit things worthy of stripes, shall be beaten with few stripes."

I think this last verse firmly establishes this doctrine of degrees of sin and punishment.

SARAH: I must admit that I'm now convinced that not all sins are equally grievous and offensive to God and that God will punish sinners differently according to the number and nature of their sins.

TOM: Could you elaborate on the phrase "some sins, in themselves, … are more heinous"?

JON: This has to do with the nature of the sin itself. Let me give some examples. I'm sure you would agree that blasphemy against God is more heinous in its own nature than speaking evil of one's neighbour. Another example is in Proverbs 6:30 and 32, where we read that adultery is more heinous than stealing to satisfy one's soul when one is hungry. In general, sins committed directly against God (the first table of the law) are more heinous than those committed directly against man (the second table of the law). As an aside, I once heard a man trying to justify his adulterous relationship by reasoning in this manner: "Jesus taught that it is a sin to look at a woman lustfully; the very thought of which is considered committing adultery with her in the heart. Now, since I've already had lustful thoughts about a certain woman, I might as well just go ahead with the actual physical act of adultery. After all, it really doesn't matter whether I commit this sin physically or mentally since I would have broken the seventh commandment anyway." Tom, what do you make of such reasoning?

TOM: First, a man who reasons in this way simply can't be a true believer! In fact, the moment he realises he has committed this sin in his heart, he ought immediately to repent of it and beg the Lord for forgiveness. He shouldn't even be thinking of how he might proceed further in his wickedness! Second, he fails to realise that even though having lustful thoughts about a woman is sinful, it is not as sinful as the actual act of adultery! Furthermore, by actually committing the physical act, he is in fact adding to the number of his sins.

SARAH: What about the phrase, "Some sins...by reason of several aggravations, are more heinous"?

JON: This speaks of the circumstances surrounding a sin that make it more or less grievous. There are at least three aggravations of sin to take note of. I'll just give them very briefly, and we can think about them in our own time. First is the offender himself. For example, the sin of a parent, a teacher, a magistrate, or someone in an influential position is worse than the same sin committed by a child, a student, a subject, or someone in a subordinate position. Second is the place and time at which the sin is committed. For example, a sin committed in a public place is worse than the same sin done in secret; and a sin committed on the Sabbath is worse than the same sin committed on other days. Third is the manner in which the sin is committed. For example, a sin committed against knowledge and conscience is worse than one committed in ignorance.

SARAH: But now that we're all persuaded about the doctrine of degrees of sin and punishment, do you think that this knowledge may occasionally tempt us to justify or condone certain "lesser" sins in our life, or in the lives of others, because we think that they aren't so serious after all and may be tolerated?

TOM: I don't think so. But perhaps to steer us clear of such dangerous thoughts, we would do well to consider this question: **What doth every sin deserve?**

JON: **Every sin deserveth God's wrath and curse, both in this life, and that which is to come.** By God's wrath and curse, I mean God's punishments, which He will inflict upon all unrepentant sinners for their sins. Now these punishments may or may not be executed on the sinner in this life, but you can be absolutely sure that no sinner will ever escape them in the life to come! Furthermore, there's not one single sin, however small or insignificant it may appear to be, that will not go unpunished.

TOM: As Christians, we ought never to take the slightest sin lightly because Christ died on the cross for even the least of our sins. Instead, we ought to be ever so grateful to Him for His great work of redemption and demonstrate our gratitude by daily casting aside every weight and sin that so easily besets us and running with patience the race that is set before us (Hebrews 12:1).

JON: Well said. All right, let's stop at this point and continue next week with a discussion on the way to be saved and the means of grace.

SARAH: Hmmm, that sounds interesting. I was wondering if I could invite a very good friend of mine to our weekly meetings. You see, this friend was once a very fervent Christian during our younger days. But ever since she entered college, she experienced a season of spiritual declension, which eventually led to her dropping out of church completely. Recently, though, she called me to ask if she could come back to church once again to join us. I was delighted to hear of her desire to renew fellowship with us, and I thought it might be a good idea to encourage her further through our weekly meetings.

JON: We would be delighted to have her around! Please let her know that she's most welcome to join us.

Chapter 17

The Way of Escape (Q85-87)

Friday 7:30 p.m. (week 7)

MARY: I'm really thankful for the invitation to join you in your weekly meetings. It's been more than ten years now since I last went to church or participated in a meeting like this. Sarah and I used to be so active in church during our teenage years. But, sadly, I backslid during my college days and drifted away from the Lord and His people. These past ten years of "wilderness" wandering have been rather miserable ones. I sought for happiness in the pleasures and riches of this world, but nothing could satisfy my soul. Although life went on rather smoothly for me during those years, there seemed to be a void – a feeling of emptiness within. Then, not too long ago, while I was cleaning and clearing up my room, I came across a book that I hadn't seen in a long time. It was St Augustine's *Confessions*, which I studied as part of my classics course at college. The very first few lines of the book caught my attention: "Man is one of your creatures, Lord, and his instinct is to praise you ... The thought of you stirs him so deeply that he cannot be content unless he praises you, because you made us for yourself and our hearts find no peace until they rest in you."[32]

SARAH: Is that what made you decide to return and to seek the Lord afresh?

MARY: Yes, indeed. After reading those words, I was very much grieved in my heart as I considered my life and realised how far I had strayed from the purpose for which God has created me. I am now resolved to return to the Lord and make a fresh start to my Christian life, but it's been so long, and I'm not sure what to do or even where to begin.

JONATHAN: Well, Mary, there's no cause for despair. The same Lord who has made us for Himself also has given us directions on how He may be sought and found. Actually, I'm thrilled to hear of how God has led you (and is even now leading you!) back to Himself. And I pray that our next few weeks of discussions will be helpful to you in your road to recovery. We left off last week on a rather bleak note, namely, the penalty of the law. We said that every sin deserves God's wrath and curse both in this life and that which is to come. And since every man is a sinner, every man justly deserves to be punished by a holy and just God. Today, we want to consider the way of escape that God has graciously provided for mankind.

THOMAS: Since becoming a Christian a few weeks ago, I haven't stopped being amazed at why God would want to save sinners from their miserable and sinful state, even though they hate Him and love their sins. And I've had a great desire in my heart to tell my unbelieving friends and relatives of this good news. But somehow I don't feel confident enough to explain to them God's way of escape, or, in other words, to answer this question: **What doth God require of us, that we may escape his wrath and curse due to us for sin?**

JON: I'm glad to hear that you have such a desire to witness for Christ. Well, the answer to your question is simply this: **To escape the wrath and curse of God due to us for sin, God requireth of us faith in Jesus Christ, repentance unto life, with the diligent use of all the outward means whereby Christ communicateth to us the benefits of redemption.** There are essentially three things that God requires of us in order to escape His wrath and curse: faith, repentance, and the diligent use of all the outward means. Now the first two, faith and repentance, are what we would call inward graces. These inward graces, which the Holy Spirit works in our hearts directly, are distinguished from the outward means. This is not to say that the inward graces and the outward means are unrelated. In fact, there is a very close relationship between them. This week we'll look at faith and repentance in a little more detail, and we'll leave the outward means till next week.

SARAH: I feel a little uncomfortable with the idea that God requires of us to use the means diligently. Isn't that coming close to the idea of salvation by one's works? Aren't we having to do something to earn our salvation?

JON: Don't worry, Sarah, we're not approaching anywhere near salvation by works! Allow me to explain. We all agree that there is nothing we can do to earn salvation and to merit eternal life. Our best works are terribly bad by God's standard, and our righteousnesses are like filthy rags in His sight. Only God, through Christ, can save us. But although we can't work for or merit our salvation, nevertheless if we are to be saved, God does require of us certain things that are necessary but not meritorious. The good news is that even these things, which He requires of us, are given to us by His grace! How, then, can they merit salvation if they are but gracious gifts in the first place?

MARY: Are you saying that faith and repentance are both gifts of God?

JON: Yes, that's right; and that's what the Bible teaches. Here are two examples. Ephesians 2:8 says, "For by grace are ye saved through faith; and that not of yourselves: it is the **gift** of God:" Again in Acts 11:18 we read, "When they heard these things, they held their peace, and glorified God, saying, Then hath God also to the Gentiles **granted** repentance unto life." So we see that it is God who gives us both the ability and the willingness to believe and to repent. Left to ourselves, we can never truly believe or repent!

TOM: What about the outward means? Are they also gracious gifts?

JON: Yes, they are. In fact, these outward means are the channels God uses to communicate saving grace to us. In other words, we receive grace from God through the proper use of these means. That's the reason why the outward means are also called the means of grace!

SARAH: **What is faith in Jesus Christ?**

JON: **Faith in Jesus Christ is a saving grace, whereby we receive and rest upon Him alone for salvation, as he is offered to us in the gospel.**

MARY: Before we get into the definition of faith, I'd like to find out how faith actually saves a person.

JON: That's an important question. Many Christians today have some wrong ideas about faith. I can think of at least two of them. First, some think that faith originates from within the sinner's heart; second, some believe that faith justifies the sinner. Tom, perhaps you can comment on the first, and I'll talk about the second.

TOM: As you mentioned earlier, faith is God's gift and doesn't originate from the sinner's heart. And the reason why a sinner cannot generate true faith from within himself is because he is totally depraved by nature. He neither desires God nor seeks after Him, much less believes in Him. Furthermore, it is not enough for the Holy Spirit just to persuade the sinner to believe, because the sinner is dead in sin and unable to respond to any persuasion. It takes nothing less than the Holy Spirit's powerful work of regeneration in the sinner, giving him a new heart in order for him to respond to the gospel in faith.

JON: Excellent! The second common mistake about faith is that faith actually justifies a sinner. Tom and I spoke about this some time ago, but I'll repeat it again as I think it's quite important. This mistake really arises from a wrong idea about the doctrine of justification by faith. It's true that a sinner is justified when he exercises faith in Christ, but that does not mean that his faith is the meritorious cause of his justification. In other words, his faith is not the basis for his being justified, and it does not merit justification. Instead, the only true ground for justification is Jesus Christ, or more specifically, the work of Christ in redemption. In a sense, all of us are justified by works – not *our* works but the perfect work of Christ. Romans 3:24 states, "Being justified freely by his grace through the redemption that is in Christ Jesus."

MARY: If faith is not the *meritorious* cause of our justification, then what role does it play?

JON: Faith is the *instrumental* cause of our justification. You can think of faith as the hand that is stretched out to receive a gift or as a water pipe that channels in the water. Faith is the instrument to appropriate Christ and all the benefits of redemption that He has purchased for us.

TOM: Earlier you gave us a definition of faith. Could you expand on it further?

JON: There are essentially two elements in saving faith. The first has to do with knowing and understanding what the Bible teaches about Christ and His gospel. This would include things like who Christ is and what He has done for sinners in His life on this earth and in His death upon the cross in order to save them from their sins. It is vitally important to emphasize this, because there are many people today who believe in a "Christ" of their own making and imagination and not the Christ who is described and presented in the Bible. Such faith in a false Christ will not lead to salvation. So, for example, if you believe that Christ is a mere man and not God Himself, then you do not believe in the Christ of the Bible and you are still lost in your sins. Similarly, if you believe that Christ died on the cross merely to give mankind a wonderful example of self-sacrifice and nothing more, then you do not believe what the Bible plainly teaches about the death of Christ, and you are still lost in your sins.

MARY: Hmm, this means that a sound knowledge of the gospel is a vital component of saving faith.

JON: Yes, it is! And that is why it is important for all of us to be properly instructed in the truths of God's Word. But sound knowledge alone is not enough. And so the second element of true saving faith is a wholehearted and sincere acceptance of this knowledge concerning Christ and His gospel. It is not enough just to say that you believe in Christ. You must truly receive and rest upon Him in your heart. And so we read in Romans 10:9, "If thou shalt confess with thy mouth the Lord Jesus, and shalt believe in thine heart that God hath raised him from the dead, thou shalt be saved."

SARAH: I would like to share an illustration I once heard during a children's Sunday school class on faith, or should I say the lack of it. "A world-famous acrobat secured a cable across the Niagara River Gorge. This gorge is very wide and deep. A rough river rushes through the canyon several hundred feet below. A large crowd gathered to see this famous tightrope walker cross the Niagara Gorge by walking on this cable. First, the acrobat stood on the cable, facing the crowd, and shouted, 'Who believes that I can walk across this gorge on this cable and return?' The crowd knew that he was a famous tightrope walker, and they called back that they believed he could. When the acrobat returned, he threw down his balance rod, had a wheelbarrow lifted up onto the cable and called to the crowd, 'Who believes that I can walk across this cable and back pushing this wheelbarrow?' The crowd again expressed their belief in him. When he returned, the acrobat said, 'Who believes that I can walk across this cable pushing my wheelbarrow with a person in it?' Many waved their hands and shouted that they 'believed.' 'Okay,' said the acrobat to a 'believing' man in the front, 'you ... into the wheelbarrow!' The man stood motionless in shocked silence. He then refused to step into the wheelbarrow."[33]

JON: Excellent story! Indeed, true saving faith is not just about knowing some things or saying that you believe in them. True saving faith is a wholehearted resting and trusting in Christ to save you from your sins and to bring you safely to your heavenly home.

TOM: Let's move on to talk about the second inward grace, namely, repentance. **What is Repentance unto life?**

JON: **Repentance unto life is a saving grace, whereby a sinner out of a true sense of his sin, and apprehension of the mercy of God in Christ, doth, with grief and hatred of his sin, turn from it unto God, with full purpose of, and endeavour after, new obedience.** Repentance is not something many people today like to hear or talk about. Mary, can you think of a reason for that?

MARY: I guess it's because repentance implies sin, and no one really likes to admit that he or she is a sinner.

SARAH: You're absolutely right! Just think of the way in which we often react to those who point out our sins and faults. We tend to become defensive, and we try our very best to vindicate our actions or words instead of humbly repenting of our sins.

JON: The first thing to note about repentance is that there is both true and false, or counterfeit, repentance. True repentance leads to eternal life, while counterfeit repentance, or worldly sorrow, leads to death. This is seen in 2 Corinthians 7:10: "For godly sorrow worketh repentance to salvation not to be repented of: but the sorrow of the world worketh death."

TOM: What, then, does true repentance consist of?

JON: True repentance, or repentance unto life as the Scriptures call it, has basically two elements – a turning from sin and a turning to God. Sarah, can you identify the four elements involved in turning from sin?

SARAH: First, it involves having a true sense of one's own sin. It's one thing to know that I've sinned and quite another to actually feel it and be willing to confess it! Second, it involves realising and understanding that there is mercy with God through Jesus Christ, without whom there is absolutely no hope. Third, it involves having a sorrow for sin. Such sorrow arises not from the consequences of sin, but rather because God is greatly dishonoured by it, and Christ was crucified for it. Last, it involves a hatred for sin. Sin is to be greatly abhorred because it is the most hateful thing in God's eyes.

JON: Good! Tom, could you identify the three things involved in turning to God?

TOM: First, it involves seeking God for mercy and for the forgiveness of sins. Second, it involves making a conscious and wholehearted choice to follow God and to submit to His rule. And, third, it involves resolving to be obedient to all His commandments.

JON: Yes, that's the essence of true repentance. I want to conclude tonight's meeting by reminding us that faith and repentance are not one-time acts. These graces are to be exercised throughout our Christian life till we reach heaven, where our faith will be perfected and our repentance will no longer be necessary because we shall be made perfectly holy. Thomas Watson once wrote, "The two great graces essential to a saint in this life are faith and repentance. These are the two wings by which he flies to heaven."[34]

Chapter 18

The Means of Grace (Q88-93)

Friday 7:30 p.m. (week 8)

SARAH: Mary, how did you find our meeting last week?

MARY: I thought it was very interesting and enlightening, especially the part on saving faith! I'm looking forward to today's discussion on the outward means of grace.

JON: Glad to hear that you found our discussion profitable. As I mentioned last week, we'll take a closer look today at the outward means whereby Christ communicates to us the benefits of redemption. This subject of the outward means probably could occupy us for the next four weeks or so. But before we begin, I'd like to share something that I read yesterday as an encouragement to study this subject. The book is entitled, *Christ's Counsel to His Languishing Church* by Obadiah Sedgwick.[35] Sedgwick wrote, "And so the decaying

Christian strengthens himself when being awakened, excited, and assisted by the Spirit of Christ, he applies himself unto, and continues in the use of, all holy and raising means whether public or private, or both, until God again strengthens what He has wrought in him." And to Christians who do not find themselves in such a state of declension, he says, "Bless the arm of the Almighty God, who has given grace and upheld it ... Use all the means you can to keep up your graces, so that you sink not into a dying condition." So really, it doesn't matter what spiritual state we're in, we're called to diligently use all the means for the recovery, maintenance, and growth of our Christian life.

TOM: So what are these external means or ways that Christ uses to bring us the benefits of redemption, or **what are the outward means whereby Christ communicateth to us the benefits of redemption?**

JON: **The outward and ordinary means whereby Christ communicateth to us the benefits of redemption, are his ordinances, especially the Word, sacraments, and prayer; all which are made effectual to the elect for salvation.** There are basically three means, namely, the Word, the sacraments, and prayer. We'll look at each of them in more detail as we go along.

SARAH: What does the word "ordinary" mean in this context?

JON: The word ordinary is used in contrast to extraordinary. God has not limited Himself to using just these ordinary means to bring His elect to salvation. There are times when He uses extraordinary means! A good example from the Scriptures is the conversion of the apostle Paul, who saw an extraordinary light and heard the voice of Christ speaking to Him from heaven (Acts 9:3-8). Another example I can think of is the way in which God saves His elect who die in their infant years or who are mentally incapable of understanding the gospel. But the ordinary and usual way in which God brings His people to salvation is through the use of these means. In other words, no person can willfully neglect the use of these means and still have good reason to think that he'll be saved. And we who are Christians cannot expect God's blessing if we neglect God's means.

SARAH: How I pray that Christians today would have such a high view of the means of grace! I know of too many Christians who think that they can grow in grace even though they constantly neglect the means of grace! Truly, if we are to seek God, we must seek Him in the right way, in the way that He has appointed and ordained, and not in any way we like.

TOM: I must confess that I'm not comfortable with the fact that the sacraments are included as one of the means God uses to make the salvation of the elect effectual. Are you somehow implying that the church should also allow unbelieving people who are seeking God to make use of the sacraments?

JON: No, not at all. We'll look more carefully at the sacraments later on and see who should use them. But for now, I think I know why you're feeling a little uncomfortable. Let me try to clarify. We must understand that the idea of salvation should not be equated solely with one's conversion, which occurs at a particular point in time. When we speak of salvation here, we include all the other aspects of it too, such as regeneration, sanctification, and glorification. In fact, there is a sense in which our salvation at this present time is not yet complete while we undergo the process of sanctification and await the perfecting of our bodies and souls, which only occur will at the resurrection. All of us are still being saved each day! I once heard someone say, "The best way to know that you're saved is to know that you're being saved!" I couldn't agree more.

TOM: Thanks. That was helpful. I've been accustomed to thinking of salvation as a single event in time rather than as a process.

SARAH: Let's now look at the first means of grace, the Word of God. **How is the Word made effectual to salvation?**

JON: **The Spirit of God maketh the reading, but especially the preaching of the Word, an effectual means of convincing and converting sinners, and of building them up in holiness and comfort, through faith, unto salvation.** When I talk about the Word, I'm really referring to the whole of the Scriptures, both Old and New Testaments. Notice that the Scriptures, and especially the sound and faithful preaching of them, have two uses – the conversion of sinners and the building up of saints. In other words, both Christians and non-Christians need God's Word.

MARY: When you use the phrase "especially the preaching," are you saying that it is more important for us to listen to someone preach God's Word than to actually read it for ourselves?

JON: Well, first, both the reading and hearing of God's Word become useful to one's salvation only when the Spirit of God works in one's heart through these means. That's the reason why no amount of persuasion, reasoning, and arguments (regardless of how convincing they may be) can ever make an unbeliever believe that the Scripture is the Word of God. It takes nothing less than the inward work of the Holy Spirit to do it. And so a person without the Holy Spirit's working may read the Bible a hundred times and listen to a thousand sermons, but it will all be useless. Second, Scripture teaches us that God is especially pleased to use the instrument of preaching, more than anything else, to save souls as well as to give understanding to His people. Let's look at two examples. Romans 10:14 says, "How then shall they call on him in whom they have not believed? and how shall they believe in him of whom they have not heard? and how shall they hear without a preacher?" And 1 Corinthians 1:21 states, "It pleased God by the foolishness of preaching to save them that believe." You know, people today don't think very highly of preaching. It is foolishness to them. Even Christians don't have much patience for it. But that doesn't change the fact that God has always used preaching as the primary means, even in the Old Testament, to bring His people to salvation. To summarise, God speaks to us as we read His Word privately, and none of us should neglect reading our Bibles everyday. But remember that it is especially through the preaching of God's Word that we hear His voice most clearly and powerfully.

TOM: How does the Word of God convert sinners?

JON: God's Word enlightens and convinces them of their sinful state before a Holy God, humbles them when they realise that they are unable to save themselves, and finally drives them to Christ for their salvation.

SARAH: How about Christians? How does the Word build us up?

JON: The Word builds us up in two ways: in holiness and in comfort. I'll just point out two verses that show this clearly. In 2 Timothy 3:16 Paul writes, "All scripture is given by inspiration of God, and is profitable for doctrine, for reproof, for correction, for instruction in righteousness." And we read in Romans 15:4, "For whatsoever things were written aforetime were written for our learning, that we through patience and comfort of the scriptures might have hope."

MARY: **How is the Word to be read and heard, that it may become effectual to salvation?**

JON: That's a very important and practical question. And it's something of which we need to remind ourselves every time we come to God's Word. **That the Word**

may become effectual to salvation, we must attend thereunto with diligence, preparation, and prayer; receive it with faith and love, lay it up in our hearts, and practise it in our lives. We can see in this answer the things we ought to do *before, during,* and *after* reading or hearing the Word.

TOM: How should we prepare ourselves before receiving the Word?

JON: First, we should consider who God is. He is the most majestic, holy, and sovereign one in the entire universe, and it is His Word that we are about to receive. Second, we should examine ourselves to see if there are any sins in our lives and repent of them, because sin is a great hindrance to the receiving of His Word. James 1:21 says, "Wherefore lay apart all filthiness and superfluity of naughtiness, and receive with meekness the engrafted word, which is able to save your souls." Third, we must pray for God's assistance and blessing in making the Word effectual to us by His Spirit's working.

SARAH: What should we do when receiving the Word?

JON: First, we should give it our best attention and diligently listen to all that it has to say. Second, we must mix our hearing of it with faith, receiving all that it says with a wholehearted trust. Hebrews 4:2 warns against unbelief when attending to God's Word: "But the word preached did not profit them, not being mixed with faith in them that heard it." Third, we must receive it with love because it is the Word of God (2 Thessalonians 2:10b).

MARY: What should we do after reading or hearing God's Word?

JON: We must hide it in our hearts like a precious treasure. The psalmist says in Psalm 119:11, "Thy word have I hid in mine heart, that I might not sin against thee." And we must practise what we've learned. We sometimes lament that we can't remember what we've learned from God's Word. Well, may I suggest that the best way to remember it is to apply it to our lives! After all, it's harder to forget something when you actually do it. Okay, let's move on to the next means of grace – the sacraments.

TOM: **How do the sacraments become effectual means of salvation?**

JON: **The sacraments become effectual means of salvation, not from any virtue in them, or in him that doth administer them, but only by the blessing of Christ, and the working of his Spirit in them that by faith receive them.** There are a few things we should know about the way in which the sacraments become means of grace. First, the sacraments, in themselves, do not contain any goodness or power so as to give grace to the recipients of them. Second, the effectiveness of a sacrament is not dependent upon the person administering it; and neither does the person administering the sacrament have any power to confer grace upon those who receive it. Third, and on a positive note, the sacraments become effectual means of salvation only by the blessing and presence of Christ, and by the working of the Spirit in the hearts of those who receive it.

SARAH: We've mentioned the word *sacrament* quite a few times already, but **what is a sacrament?**

JON: **A sacrament is an holy ordinance instituted by Christ, wherein, by sensible signs, Christ, and the benefits of the new covenant, are represented, sealed, and applied to believers.** We note four things about a sacrament. First, it must be instituted and appointed by Christ alone, and not by anyone else, not even the church. Second, the sacrament is like a sign that represents something. It is an outward and visible representation of an inward and invisible work of God's grace. It is called a sensible sign because it can be sensed and experienced by our physical senses. Third, the sacrament is an official seal that God uses to visibly certify and confirm what has been signified. God binds Himself, by a sensible and authoritative seal, to give us what has been signified in the sacrament if we believe and obey Him. And on our part, when we receive the sacrament, we bind ourselves to fulfill all the duties implied in the gospel. Fourth, the sacrament actually applies to believers those things that are signified in the sacrament. In other words, the sacrament is an instrument of God to give us grace and to bless us.

SARAH: What are the things signified by the outward sign of a sacrament?

JON: The outward sign of a sacrament signifies Christ and the benefits of the new covenant.

TOM: I once heard someone say that the sacrament is a kind of visible sermon used to teach deep spiritual truths by outward signs.

JON: That's right! The sacraments give us a visible picture of the work of God's grace within us. One theologian puts it this way: "The truth addressed to the ear in the Word, is symbolically represented to the eye in the sacraments."[36] But I would like us to take note of two important things. First, although the sacraments are, as you said, visible sermons, they are never complete without the Word of God. In fact, a sacrament ceases to be a sacrament if it is separated from the preached Word. The Word of God can stand by itself without the sacrament, but never the other way round. Second, the sacraments are not merely outward representing signs; they are also inward spiritual seals that confirm and apply Christ and the benefits of the new covenant. There is a very close connection between the sign, which is outward and visible, and the thing signified, which is inward and spiritual. And so, when we receive the sacraments in a right manner, namely, by faith, then God's grace actually accompanies it. The external sign thus becomes a means by which the Holy Spirit gives us inward grace. Thomas Vincent puts it this way: "When the minister doth give forth the signs or outward elements, in the sacramental action, the Lord doth give forth and convey the things signified unto the worthy receivers."[37]

MARY: One last question: **Which are the sacraments of the New Testament?**

JON: **The sacraments of the New Testament are, Baptism, and the Lord's Supper.** We'll wait till next week to look at them in more detail.

Chapter 19

Baptism and the Lord's Supper (Q94-97)

Friday 7:30 p.m. (week 9)

THOMAS: Before we begin today's discussion on baptism and the Lord's Supper, I do have a question to ask.

JONATHAN: Go ahead.

TOM: I checked in the concordance a few days ago and discovered that the word *sacrament* isn't found anywhere in the Bible. Don't you think it would be better if we used biblical terminology instead, like *ordinance,* which appears almost thirty times in the Bible?

JON: Good question. In fact, many Protestant churches prefer not to use the word *sacrament* because of its association with Roman Catholicism. But let's look at what the word actually means. The word *sacrament* is derived from the Latin word *sacramentum,* which carries the idea of a sacred or divine secret. If you think about it, there is indeed an element of secrecy and mystery about the sacraments. This is seen from the fact that the spiritual significance and blessing of a sacrament is hidden under the external symbol and ritual of the sacrament. Furthermore, during the days when the early church suffered great persecution from the Romans, Christians had to observe the sacraments in secrecy. That's probably another reason why the early Christians used this word to describe the two ordinances. But there is another interesting fact about the word *sacrament* that makes it a suitable word to use. The dictionary meaning of a sacrament is an oath of allegiance taken by newly enlisted soldiers. In ancient times, when a solider made a *sacramentum*, he engaged himself to be faithful to his commander. Similarly, as Christians, when we receive the sacraments, we engage ourselves to be the Lord's and to be faithful to Him.

SARAH: Interesting, indeed! Actually, I was thinking that as long as the things signified by a particular word are scriptural, it shouldn't be improper to use that word even though it isn't found in the Scriptures. Another example would be the word *trinity,* which is not found in Bible, but we use it regularly.

MARY: Jon, you mentioned last week that there are two sacraments in the New Testament. How about the about Old Testament? Were there sacraments there? And if so, what were they?

JON: Yes, there certainly were sacraments in the Old Testament. The two most common and important ones were circumcision and the Passover. Whereas the New Testament sacraments point to Christ, who had already come and completed His earthly ministry, the Old Testament sacraments pointed to the same Christ, who was yet to come. There are similarities and differences between the Old and New Testament sacraments, which we'll look at later. For now, we should simply note that in terms of the spiritual things signified and applied, the sacraments of the Old and New Testament are the same.

TOM: That's something new and interesting. I never realised that the sacraments of baptism and the Lord's Supper actually have their roots in the Old Testament! Let's start with the first one: **What is Baptism?**

JON: **Baptism is a sacrament, wherein the washing with water, in the name of the Father, and of the Son, and of the Holy Ghost, doth signify and seal our ingrafting into Christ, and partaking of the benefits of the covenant of grace, and our engagement to be the Lord's.** First of all, let me say that baptism is a huge topic, and we won't have time to cover every aspect of it in detail. Furthermore, through the ages and especially in our age, the church has been divided on three issues relating to baptism, namely, *how* a person is to be baptised, *why* a person is baptised, and *who* is to be baptised. I don't wish to enter into the controversies for now. We can leave that to a later time, or you can read up on it for yourself.[38] Instead, I hope to briefly state what I believe to be the scriptural truths concerning baptism.

169

MARY: What is the purpose for baptism?

JON: There are a number of purposes, but I'll highlight just three important ones. First, baptism is for the purpose of signifying and sealing our ingrafting or joining to Christ. We who were once alienated from Christ because of sin are now united with Him and made members of His body. This union with Christ occurred when the Holy Spirit changed our hearts at regeneration and worked faith in us so that we were able and willing to embrace Christ as our Saviour. All those who are thus joined to Christ are identified with Him and are saved from condemnation, just as those who were identified with Noah were saved from that great flood. Our outward water baptism points to an inward spiritual baptism by the Holy Spirit. First Corinthians 12:13 says, "For by one Spirit are we all baptized into one body, whether we be Jews or Gentiles, whether we be bond or free; and have been all made to drink into one Spirit."

TOM: What's the second purpose for baptism?

JON: Baptism is a sign and seal of the covenant of grace, as well as of our partaking in the benefits of that covenant. This is so because baptism has now replaced circumcision as the New Testament sign and seal of the covenant of grace.

SARAH: How do we know that?

JON: To start with, let's look at the purpose of circumcision in the Old Testament. Circumcision was first instituted back in Genesis 17:10, when God declared

His covenant with Abraham. God said, "This is my covenant, which ye shall keep, between me and you and thy seed after thee; Every man child among you shall be circumcised." Note that the covenant mentioned in Genesis 17, also known as the Abrahamic covenant, comes under the umbrella of the covenant of grace. The "everlasting covenant" of Genesis 17:7 in the Old Testament is the same "everlasting covenant" of Hebrews 13:20 in the New Testament. We mustn't view them as separate covenants. Circumcision was the sign and seal of the covenant of grace in the Old Testament (Romans 4:11-12 confirms this). In other words, physical circumcision pointed to real or actual circumcision, which is of the heart. There are a number of Old Testament passages that speak of the circumcision of the heart, and they show us that "heart" circumcision was what mattered most (e.g., Leviticus 26:40-41; Deuteronomy 10:16; 30:6). And in the New Testament, Paul tells us that it is "heart" circumcision and not physical circumcision that determines whether a person is a true believer or not. Romans 2:28-29 says, "For he is not a Jew, which is one outwardly; neither is that circumcision, which is outward in the flesh: But he is a Jew, which is one inwardly; and circumcision is that of the heart." And then in that remarkable passage in Colossians 2:11-12, Paul shows us that physical circumcision is unnecessary for us today because we, who have been spiritually circumcised (i.e., circumcised in our hearts) have already had our spiritual circumcision, signified by water baptism. Now, if physical circumcision was used in the Old Testament to point to "heart" circumcision; and baptism, in the New Testament, also signifies heart circumcision, then isn't it true that the outward rites of circumcision and baptism both point to the same inward grace and that the latter has replaced the former?

SARAH: Hmm -- interesting!

MARY: What are the benefits of the covenant of grace that are signified and sealed by baptism?

JON: I can think of at least four: forgiveness of sins through Christ's blood (Mark 1:4; Acts 2:38), regeneration and sanctification by Christ's Spirit (Titus 3:5), adoption (Galatians 3:26-4:5), and resurrection to everlasting life (Romans 6:4-5).

MARY: How about the third purpose for baptism?

JON: The third purpose for baptism is to signify and seal our vow and engagement to be wholly and only the Lord's. In other words, baptism is an open declaration that we belong to the Lord and that we seek to walk in the newness of life. Romans 6:4 declares, "Therefore we are buried with him by baptism into death: that like as Christ was raised up from the dead by the glory of the Father, even so we also should walk in newness of life."

SARAH: Who should be baptized then? **To whom is baptism to be administered?**

JON: **Baptism is not to be administered to any that are out of the visible church, till they profess their faith in Christ, and obedience to him; but the infants of such as are members of the visible church are to be baptised.** There are basically two groups of people that should be baptized – those who profess to be Christians and infants of believers. When a person is baptized, whether infant or adult, he or she is recognised by fellow believers to be a member of the visible church, and the church is to treat such a person as one of its members. In fact, water baptism is the only divinely appointed means for the church to admit a person into its membership.

TOM: I think I'm beginning to understand why infants also should be baptized. If baptism replaces circumcision as the sign and seal of the covenant of grace in the New Testament, then infants, who were previously circumcised in the Old Testament, should now be baptized.

JON: That's right. Remember that the promises of God made to His people extend also to their children. Genesis 17:7, "And I will establish my covenant between me and thee and thy seed after thee in their generations for an everlasting covenant, to be a God unto thee, and to thy seed after thee." Peter, when referring to the promise of the Abrahamic covenant, said in Acts 2:39, "For the promise is unto you, and to your children, and to all that are afar off, even as many as the Lord our God shall call." And so we see that children of believers, whether in the Old or New Testament, are included in the covenant too and have a right to receive the covenant sign and seal.[39]

SARAH: I still have some doubts and questions on baptism, but I would like to spend more time thinking about them first before getting back to you. Meanwhile, let's move on to the second sacrament of the New Testament. **What is the Lord's supper?**

JON: **The Lord's supper is a sacrament, wherein, by giving and receiving bread and wine, according to Christ's appointment, his death is showed forth; and the worthy receivers are, not after a corporal and carnal manner, but by faith, made partakers of his body and blood, with all his benefits, to their spiritual nourishment, and growth in grace.** The Lord's Supper, which gets its name from 1 Corinthians 11:20, is sometimes called the Breaking of Bread (Acts 2:42), or Communion (1 Corinthians 10:16). Christ first instituted it by using the elements of the Passover meal, the same night in which He was betrayed while He and the disciples were gathered in the upper room to observe the Passover. This transition from the Old Testament sacrament of the Passover to the New Testament sacrament of the Lord's Supper indicates a very close connection between the two. In fact, Paul says in 1 Corinthians 5:7, "For even Christ our passover is sacrificed for us." The Puritan Richard Vines, in his sermon on the Lord's Supper, said, "In the Passover, the sufferings and death of Christ were represented by a lamb slain and roasted with fire. In the (Lord's) Supper, they are represented by bread broken and wine poured forth. The outward symbols and signs differ, but Christ is the same under both. As circumcision was theirs and baptism ours, there are different signs and rites, but the inward circumcision and regeneration are both one. Theirs were both bloody sacraments, for the blood of Christ was to be shed; ours is unbloody, for the blood has been shed."[40]

TOM: It's fascinating to see how baptism is linked to circumcision and the Lord's Supper to the Passover!

What are the purposes for which the Lord's Supper was instituted?

JON: There are at least three of them: First, it is a sign pointing to the Lord's death (1 Corinthians 11:26), which was a sacrificial one on behalf of His people. In the Old Testament, the sacrifices prefigured Christ, while in the New Testament this sacrament points back to the same Christ, who has already been sacrificed. The death of Christ is really the most important event in all of redemptive history, and the Lord's Supper is to be a reminder of it.

SARAH: I'm surprised that there are other purposes for which this sacrament was instituted, apart from the one you just mentioned. I've always thought that the Lord's Supper is to be nothing more than a commemoration or memorial of the Lord's death as taught in 1 Corinthians 11:25-26.

JON: Well, it certainly is that, but it's also more than that. Remember that a sacrament, as we saw last week, not only acts as an outward sign; it also seals and applies to us Christ and the benefits of the new covenant. And so, the second purpose for which the Lord's Supper was instituted is to be a seal to confirm our participation in the crucified Christ and all the benefits that His death has purchased for us. As a seal, the Lord's Supper both exhibits and affirms the reality and "genuineness" of our redemption in Christ. The third purpose for the Lord's Supper is to be a means of spiritual nourishment for our hungry souls. Just as our bodies derive physical nourishment from the food we eat, so also do our souls derive spiritual nourishment from the right use of this sacrament. Take note that though Christ is not present literally and physically in the elements of the Lord's Supper, He is present spiritually. When we receive the bread and the wine, we actually feed on Him in a spiritual manner.[41]

TOM: That's a real mystery indeed! Could you give us some benefits of receiving the Lord's Supper in a right manner?

JON: Well, first, our faith in Christ and repentance unto life (the two graces we exercised at conversion) are further exercised and renewed when we come to the Lord's Table. Second, our assurance of God's love grows when we are reminded and assured that all the promises of the covenant of grace and the riches of the gospel are ours and that we have a personal claim on them. Richard Vines writes, "So if doubts arise concerning the reality of God and the sureness of this covenant that speaks of so much grace and mercy, we look upon and take hold of this seal of blood, and are thereby settled and therein acquiesce."[42] Third, we are strengthened in our resolve to be faithful servants of our King. Whenever we eat the bread and drink the cup, we declare our allegiance to Christ and solemnly pledge to live a life of obedience to Him.

MARY: What is the right and proper way of receiving the Lord's Supper? **What is required to the worthy receiving of the Lord's supper?**

JON: **It is required of them that would worthily partake of the Lord's supper, that they examine themselves of their knowledge to discern the Lord's body, of their faith to feed upon him, of their repentance, love, and new obedience; lest coming unworthily, they eat and drink judgment to themselves.** First Corinthians 11:28 says, "But let a man examine himself, and so let him eat of that bread, and drink of that cup." So before coming to the Lord's Table, we are to examine:

1) Our knowledge to discern the Lord's body – whether we understand what the Lord's death means and what the elements in the Supper represent.
2) Our faith to feed upon Him – whether we believe that Christ alone is able to save, sustain, and preserve us.
3) Our repentance – whether we have truly repented of our sins.
4) Our love – whether we sincerely love Him and His people.
5) Our new obedience – whether we resolve, in His strength, to walk as His people.

On this topic of examining ourselves, I would highly recommend Joseph Alleine's sermon entitled, "Self-Examination."[43]

SARAH: But how can we make ourselves worthy, seeing that we are all such unworthy creatures?

JON: We can't. In fact, the only ones who are "worthy" to receive the Lord's Supper are those who realise that they are utterly unworthy, in themselves, to stand before God, and thus they rest entirely upon Christ alone for their salvation! On the other hand, those who are arrogant, proud, and self-sufficient and refuse to humbly examine themselves before the Lord should stay far away from the Lord's Table, lest they provoke God to inflict physical, spiritual, or even eternal judgment on them.

TOM: I must say that I'm really looking forward to my baptism in three weeks' time and to my participation at the Lord's Table thereafter.

JON: Glad to hear that. I'm sure we'll all make every effort to be present at your baptism.

TOM: Thanks!

Chapter 20

Prayer (Part I, Q98-102)

Friday 7:30 p.m. (week 10)

JONATHAN: We've finally arrived at our last topic – prayer.

SARAH: I think we've come quite a long way in our discussions these past few weeks. We started out by looking at the duty that God requires of man, namely, obedience to the moral law, and we spent a few weeks discussing the Ten Commandments. At the end of that discussion, we saw that no mere man is able to obey God's law perfectly. Then we proceeded to talk about the things that God requires of us so that we may escape His wrath and curse due to us for our sin, namely, faith in Jesus Christ, repentance unto life, and the diligent use of all the outward means. We saw that there are three very important outward means that Christ ordinarily uses to communicate to us the benefits of redemption: the Word, the sacraments (baptism and the Lord's Supper), and prayer.

THOMAS: Thanks, Sarah, for that helpful summary. I was

just about to ask how the topic of prayer is connected with our initial discussion of God's law exactly nine weeks ago! Just recently, I visited a Christian bookstore in central London, and I was amazed at the number of books on prayer. It seems to me that prayer is a very vital and essential aspect of the Christian life. Some people have likened the exercise of prayer to breathing. Now if prayer is to a Christian what breathing is to a human being, then no Christian can afford to neglect it and still hope to survive spiritually.

SARAH: I'm sure all Christians have at least some idea of what prayer is, but I think it'll be good for us to start off with a formal definition of it. **What is prayer?**

JON: **Prayer is an offering up of our desires unto God for things agreeable to his will, in the name of Christ, with confession of our sins, and thankful acknowledgment of his mercies.** As we look at this definition, it's helpful to ask three basic questions. First, *who* are we to pray to? Second, *how* are we to pray? And, third, *what* are we to pray for? Perhaps each of you could take one question.

MARY: I'll start with the first. Prayer is to be made to God alone and no one else. I can think of a few reasons why this is so. First, there is only one true and living God, and there is no one else who is worthy to receive our prayers except Him. Second, God alone is present everywhere all the time and is able to hear our prayers wherever and whenever we cry to Him. Third, only the all-powerful God is able to answer all our prayers. Last, God Himself has instructed us in His Word to call upon Him.

JON: Good. Just two days ago, I was reading the first chapter of 2 Kings, and I came across this verse in which God rebuked King Ahaziah for seeking other gods. He said to Ahaziah, through the prophet Elijah, "Is it not because there is not a God in Israel, that ye go to inquire of Baal-zebub the god of Ekron?" (1:3). I'm reminded once again that it is a great insult to God to pray to false gods (whatever form they may take) and that He is greatly offended by this sin.

SARAH: I'll take the second question on *how* we are to pray. We are to pray in the name of Christ. I suspect many Christians today use the name of Christ in a somewhat superstitious manner, as if the mere utterance of it had some "magical" powers whenever it is used in prayer. I once had a friend who told me that if I didn't conclude my prayer with Jesus' name, then all that I had prayed for in that prayer would not be heard by God! I don't quite agree with that. I believe that praying in Christ's name means that we are to mention His name by faith, depending fully upon Him alone for acceptance with God, and for access before His throne of grace. It is to pray with full assurance that God will receive our prayers on the basis of what Christ has done for us as our Redeemer, as Ephesians 3:12 says: "In whom [Christ] we have boldness and access with confidence by the faith of him."

JON: I fully agree with you! Tom, looks like you're left with the third question: *what* are we to pray for?

181

TOM: Well, first, we are to confess our sins before the Lord. In Psalm 32:5 David sets us an example when he prayed, "I acknowledged my sin unto thee, and mine iniquity have I not hid. I said, I will confess my transgressions unto the LORD; and thou forgavest the iniquity of my sin." I notice that Christians today don't spend much time confessing their sins when they pray. Often, confession of sin is neglected altogether. I think we really need to return to this element of prayer when we pray. Second, we should give thanks for all His mercies towards us, both in temporal and in spiritual things. Third, we are to pray for those things that are agreeable to His will. We see this stated negatively in James 4:3, "Ye ask, and receive not, because ye ask amiss," and positively in 1 John 5:14, "And this is the confidence that we have in him, that, if we ask any thing according to his will, he heareth us." But how do we know what things are agreeable to His will? What guidelines should we use in prayer? **What rule hath God given for our direction in prayer?**

JON: **The whole Word of God is of use to direct us in prayer; but the special rule of direction is that form of prayer which Christ taught his disciples, commonly called the Lord's Prayer.** All of God's Word is useful in instructing and directing us in our prayers. For example, there are a quite a few records of the prayers of faithful saints in the Scriptures, and we would do well to study and learn from them. But it is in the Lord's Prayer that God gives us a special rule for prayer, and so we will study it in a little more detail. From the earliest times, it was called the Lord's Prayer because it is the Lord Jesus Christ's instruction to us on how to pray. He is the most suitable person to teach us how to pray because as our Mediator He knows exactly what our needs are and what the will of God is for us. We must therefore pay special attention to His instruction on prayer.

MARY: But how are we to use the Lord's Prayer? Are we to simply repeat the exact words whenever we pray?

JON: No, not really. You see, what we have here is a pattern or model of prayer. Now there's nothing wrong with reciting the exact words of this prayer regularly in a reverent and meaningful manner. In fact, I would encourage you to do so. But I also must warn against simply repeating the words of this prayer over and over again as a matter of habit without really meaning what we say. Instead, we are to use the Lord's Prayer as an outline and frame our prayers after its pattern. Just as a builder builds the house according to its architectural drawings, so we should build our prayers according to the pattern set for us in the Lord's Prayer.

TOM: How many parts are there in the Lord's Prayer?

JON: There are essentially three parts: a preface or introduction, several petitions, and a conclusion.

SARAH: Let's begin with the first part. **What doth the preface of the Lord's Prayer teach us?**

JON: **The preface of the Lord's Prayer, (which is, Our Father which art in heaven,) teacheth us to draw near to God with all holy reverence and confidence, as children to a father, able and ready to help us; and that we should pray with and for others.** This opening statement teaches us three things. First, we are reminded that whenever we pray, we come before a most holy and awesome God, who dwells in the highest heaven. Isaiah 57:15 says, "For thus saith the high and lofty One that inhabiteth eternity, whose name is Holy; I dwell in the high and holy place." We must never treat God lightly as if He were nothing more than a good friend on level terms with us. Second, although the distance between God and us is very great, we are nevertheless encouraged to draw near to Him with confidence as to a loving father who is ready, willing, and able to help us. Third, the words "Our Father" teach us to pray with and for others. This is important because by nature, we tend forget about the needs of others and seek only our own things.

TOM: Who are we to pray for?

JON: We are to pray for all sorts of people, for kings and magistrates, for our family members, for our church, for our friends, and even for our enemies. But we are not to pray for the dead and for those who have committed the unpardonable sin (1 John 5:16).

MARY: And who are we to pray with?

JON: We are to pray with our fellow brothers and sisters in Christ and with the church as a whole. This is why it is important for us, as much as possible, to attend the midweek church prayer meetings as they give us the opportunity to pray together with the church.

SARAH: **What do we pray for in the first petition?**

JON: **In the first petition, (which is, Hallowed be thy name,) we pray, That God would enable us and others to glorify him in all that whereby he maketh himself known; and that he would dispose all things to his own glory.**

MARY: As an aside, how many petitions are there altogether?

JON: There are six in total, although I do know of people who prefer to divide the last petition into two, and so they end up with seven altogether. Coming back to the first petition, we note that to hallow something is to set it apart for sacred use. And so in this petition, we pray that God would set apart and sanctify His own name by working all things for His own glory. Also, we pray that He would enable us and others to glorify His name in all areas of our lives. Remember that God's name is not restricted to His titles alone but encompasses His attributes, His works, and His Word. We talked about this some weeks ago when we were looking at the third commandment.

TOM: It's interesting to note that if man's chief and highest end is to glorify God, then it shouldn't surprise us that the Lord Jesus should teach us to begin our prayers by seeking first His glory.

JON: That's right. And by beginning our prayers in this manner, we are giving God the supreme place and acknowledging that we desire His glory above all our other needs and requests. Before we go on, I'd like to share a few lines from David Brainerd's diary, which I treasure very much. Brainerd was a missionary to the North American Indians during the eighteenth century. Towards the end of his life (and he died at age 29) as he lay on his bed in great agony due to his illness, he said, "My heaven is to please God, and glorify Him, and to give all to Him, and to be wholly devoted to His glory. That is the heaven I long for; that is my religion, and that is my happiness … I do not go to heaven to be advanced, but to give honour to God. It is no matter where I shall be stationed in heaven, whether I have a high or low seat there; but to love, and please, and glorify God is all."[44]

MARY: Beautiful words indeed! We're living in an age where selfishness and pride are great "virtues"; how we need more of such reminders and encouragements to seek God's glory above all else.

TOM: **What do we pray for in the second petition?**

JON: **In the second petition, (which is, Thy kingdom come,) we pray, That Satan's kingdom may be destroyed; and that the kingdom of grace may be advanced, ourselves and others brought into it, and kept in it; and that the kingdom of glory may be hastened.** The first petition has to do with the glory of God. The second and third petitions have to do with the way in which God's glory is to be manifested and promoted in this world.

MARY: What does Satan's kingdom refer to?

JON: Satan's kingdom simply refers to all the powers of this universe that stand in opposition to God, such as false teachings and religions; anti-Christian governments and authorities that oppose Christ and persecute His people; cultures and worldly systems that seek to draw people away from God through various means; and the corruption of our own nature, which wars against our spirit (Romans 7:23). We are to pray that this kingdom may be destroyed. As Thomas Watson says, "Let us pray that Satan's kingdom, set up in the world, may be overthrown. It is sad to think that, though the devil's kingdom be so bad, yet that it should have so many to support it … Satan's kingdom must be thrown down before Christ's kingdom can flourish in its power and majesty."[45]

SARAH: Earlier, you spoke of Christ's kingdom in two parts – the kingdom of grace and the kingdom of glory. What do they each mean?

JON: Well, the first speaks of His reign of grace within the hearts of His people. This is what Jesus was referring to in Luke 17:21, when He said, "For, behold, the kingdom of God is within you." Such a kingdom is a spiritual kingdom as opposed to a merely physical or political one. God rules His people from within them by His Spirit and enables them to do His will. It is called a kingdom of

187

grace because the Holy Spirit first begins a work of grace in the hearts of His people at regeneration and continues to build them up in grace through the process of sanctification. When we pray, "Thy kingdom come," we're essentially asking God to bring us and others into His gracious kingdom and to keep us in it by strengthening and establishing His work of grace in us.

TOM: How about the kingdom of glory?

JON: The kingdom of glory speaks of that glorious and everlasting kingdom that Christ shall establish in the future when He comes again. At that time, we shall behold Him in all His splendor and glory, and we shall be transformed into His image. And so when we pray this second petition, we are expressing our heart's desire for Christ to hasten the great day of His return – the day in which He shall judge the world and vindicate His saints. "Even so, come, Lord Jesus" (Revelation 22:20).

Chapter 21

Prayer (Part II, Q103-107)

F riday 7:30 p.m. (week 11)

SARAH: Tonight is our final session together, and I would like to say that I've enjoyed this series of meetings, and I hope that we'll have more of them in the future.

MARY: Me too!

JONATHAN: Well, perhaps we can start thinking of topics that we would like to discuss together; and we can always arrange to meet again.

THOMAS: I do have a few in mind already – baptism, eschatology (doctrine of last things), God's sovereignty in redemption, and biblical worship, just to name a few.

JON: Sounds interesting indeed! But for now, let's return to our discussion on prayer. We ended our meeting last week with the second petition of the Lord's Prayer. Today, we'll look at the next four petitions, together with the conclusion of this prayer.

MARY: I was thinking about the second petition and how when we pray, "Thy kingdom come," we are, among other things, praying that others may be brought into His kingdom of grace, that is, to be converted. But if God has predestined from eternity all those who will be saved, why should we pray for anyone's salvation in the first place? And taking a step back, why should we even pray for anything since God has decreed all things and prayer doesn't change anything?

JON: Good question. Some Christians would simply say that prayer does indeed change the way God works and that God cannot do certain things if we do not pray. I think the problem is that these people have a low view of God and a high view of man. If God has to change His plans and decrees based on the way we pray or act, then God is no longer sovereign. Instead, He has become subordinate to His creatures! Furthermore, if God's plans and purposes could be changed based on His reaction to our prayers, then we would have reason to doubt the wisdom and goodness of God in the first place! No, the Scriptures tell us in various passages that God is absolutely sovereign. Daniel 4:35 says, "He doeth according to his will in the army of heaven, and among the inhabitants of the earth: and none can stay his hand, or say unto him, What doest thou?" Psalm 135:6 states, "Whatsoever the LORD pleased, that did he in heaven, and in earth, in the seas, and all deep places." And in Job 23:13 Job said, "But he is in one mind, and who can turn him? And what his soul desireth, even that he doeth." We should look at prayer in this way: From God's eternal perspective, prayers changes nothing; but from a man's temporal perspective, things may seem to change because of his prayers. Let's not forget that God, who has decreed the end of all things, also has decreed the means for the working out of His decrees, and prayer is one of these means. Think about it: even our prayers are included in His eternal decrees! Isn't that amazing? I like what A. W. Pink wrote concerning prayer: "Here then is the design of prayer: not that God's will may be *altered*, but that it may be accomplished in His own good time and way. It is because God has promised certain things that we can ask for them with full assurance of faith. It is God's purpose that His will shall be brought about by His own appointed means, and that He may do His people good upon His terms, and that is, by the 'means' and 'terms' of entreaty and supplication ... Prayer is not so much an act as it is an attitude – an *attitude* of *dependency*, dependency upon God."[46]

TOM: **What do we pray for in the third petition?**

JON: **In the third petition, (which is, Thy will be done in earth, as it is in heaven,) we pray, That God, by his grace, would make us able and willing to know, obey, and submit to his will in all things, as the angels do in heaven.**

SARAH: What is meant by God's will?

JON: There are two aspects of God's will – His secret will and His revealed will. We see this distinction in Deuteronomy 29:29: "The secret *things* belong unto the LORD our God: but those *things* which are revealed belong unto us and to our children for ever, that we may do all the words of this law." The secret will of God refers to those things God has decreed to do but has chosen not to reveal to man. These things remain secret until God reveals them to us by way of providence. Some examples of God's secret will are whom He has chosen to save, how long we shall live on this earth, when Christ will return. The revealed will of God, on the other hand, speaks of those things that God has commanded us to do in His Word. This revealed will of God is summarised in His Ten Commandments. Note that God's secret, or decretive, will is always done, whether in heaven or on earth. However, this is not true of His revealed, or preceptive (from the word *precept*), will, which often is violated.

MARY: Allow me to summarise what this petition means. When we pray, "Thy will be done," we are praying for two things. First, we are praying for active obedience – that God would enable us to know, understand, and obey His revealed will. Second, we are praying for passive obedience – that He would enable us to willingly and cheerfully submit to His secret will, as it is revealed to us through His providence.

JON: Very good!

TOM: And what about the phrase "as it is in heaven"? What does that mean?

JON: That refers to the standard of obedience to God's will that we on earth are to aim at. In heaven, God's will is done perfectly, joyfully, and willingly by all His angels and saints. Someday, we too shall join together with that heavenly company and be perfected in our obedience to Him. But for now, we are to constantly strive towards that standard.

MARY: **What do we pray for in the fourth petition?**

JON: **In the fourth petition, (which is, Give us this day our daily bread,) we pray, That of God's free gift we may receive a competent portion of the good things of this life, and enjoy his blessing with them.**

SARAH: As an aside, I observe that the first three petitions relate to the cause of God, while the next three relate to our own needs and concerns as we live in this world. It reminds me of the way in which the Ten Commandments are divided: the first four teach us our duty towards God, while the next six teach us our duty towards man.

JON: That's a good observation. In fact, there are quite a few observable connections and similarities between the Ten Commandments and the Lord's Prayer. This shouldn't surprise us. After all, the One who gave us the Ten Commandments on Mount Sinai is really the same Person who gave us the Lord's Prayer in His Sermon on the Mount. On the former mountain, He spoke the words of the Ten Commandments in an audible voice and wrote them with His finger on two tables of stone. On the latter mountain, He spoke the words of the Lord's Prayer in His great sermon and wrote them, through His apostle, in His Word.

TOM: Coming back to the fourth petition, what does "bread" refer to?

JON: We should understand the word "bread" as a generic term that encompasses all things necessary for existence in this life. This would include food, water, clothing, shelter, health, appetite, sleep, and so on.

MARY: Are we to pray that God would give us just the bare necessities in life, or should we pray that we may enjoy a comfortable portion of these things?

JON: Well, we should pray that God would give us what He deems best for us. Proverbs 30:8b-9 is very instructive on this matter: "Give me neither poverty nor riches: feed me with food convenient for me: Lest I be full, and deny thee, and say, Who is the LORD? or lest I be poor, and steal, and take the name of God in vain." The important thing to remember is that we are utterly dependent upon God for all our needs and that everything we have comes from His gracious hand. We must never become arrogant or self-sufficient when God gives us riches to enjoy; and neither should we murmur or become discontented in whatever situation God places us. Also, we should pray for God's blessing to accompany our daily "bread." After all, what is the use of enjoying all the good things in this life without His blessing?

SARAH: It's interesting that the first of three petitions relating to our own needs (i.e., the fourth to sixth) is about our bodies rather than our souls. Isn't the soul more important than our bodies?

JON: The Bible commentator Matthew Henry answers your question: "Because our natural being is necessary to our spiritual well being in this world, therefore, after the things of God's glory, kingdom and will, we pray for the necessary supports and comforts of this present life."[47] Indeed, God gives to us the physical things so that we may glorify Him in our bodies and perform all the spiritual duties He requires of us in this life.

SARAH: **What do we pray for in the fifth petition?**

JON: **In the fifth petition, (which is, And forgive us our debts, as we forgive our debtors,) we pray, That God, for Christ's sake, would freely pardon all our sins; which we are the rather encouraged to ask, because by his grace we are enabled from the heart to forgive others.**

TOM: Is there a difference between a sin and a debt?

JON: There's no essential difference. In Luke 11:4, Christ used the word *sin* instead of *debt*. But the word *debt* does describe sin quite well. A debt arises when a person doesn't pay what he owes. In the same way, all of us are debtors to God because we owe Him perfect obedience and we haven't paid Him what is due. And just as a debtor who is unable to pay what is due is sent to prison for his nonpayment; so also, we, who owe God an infinite debt of sin, deserve to be sent to hell for all eternity. But thanks be to God, who through Jesus Christ, has graciously forgiven and cancelled our debt of sin. Our sins were nailed to the cross of Calvary, and Christ bore the

195

punishment for them on our behalf. As Ephesians 1:7 says, in Christ "we have redemption through his blood, the forgiveness of sins, according to the riches of his grace."

MARY: But if God has forgiven all our sins for Christ's sake, why then should we still utter this petition?

JON: It's true that as God's children all our debts are cancelled and we no longer owe God any payment for our sins. God sees us as righteous for Christ's sake. Nevertheless, because we're imperfect saints, we still sin against God and incur His fatherly displeasure; thus we still need His pardoning mercy. Perhaps an illustration at this point might be helpful. Think of a son who has offended his father by refusing to obey his father's instructions. The father may be greatly angered by his son's behaviour, and for a season there may even be a breach in their relationship; yet the father will neither cast his son out of his household nor deny him altogether. Instead, the father lovingly forgives and receives his son when his son realises his mistake and humbly comes to him for forgiveness.

SARAH: The phrase "as we forgive our debtors" has always made me a little uncomfortable. In fact, in Matthew 6:15, Jesus goes on to say, "But if ye forgive not men their trespasses, neither will your Father forgive your trespasses." Is Jesus telling us that we will only be forgiven according to the measure that we ourselves have forgiven others?

JON: On the surface, this may seem so, but it really isn't the case. The fact is that we can really forgive others only when we ourselves have been forgiven. We see this, for example, in Ephesians 4:32: "And be ye kind, one to another, tenderhearted, forgiving one another, even as God for Christ's sake hath forgiven you." By forgiving those who sin against us, we imitate our heavenly Father, who has forgiven us a great deal more than what we will ever be able to forgive. It is only by His grace that we are enabled to forgive others; and by forgiving others, we demonstrate that we are the ones who have been truly forgiven!

TOM: **What do we pray for in the sixth petition?**

JON: **In the sixth petition, (which is, And lead us not into temptation, but deliver us from evil,) we pray, That God would either keep us from being tempted to sin, or support and deliver us when we are tempted.** Having prayed for the forgiveness of sins in the fifth petition, we now ask the Lord, in the sixth petition, to keep us from sinning against Him in one of two ways – either that He will keep us from being tempted altogether or that He will support and deliver us from temptation, so that instead of sinning against Him, we emerge as victors over temptation.

MARY: But why should God allow us to be tempted in the first place?

JON: I can think of a few reasons. First, He allows us to be tempted so that our faith may be tried and strengthened.

James 1:3 says, "Knowing this, that the trying of your faith worketh patience." And we read in Job 23:10, "But he knoweth the way that I take: when he hath tried me, I shall come forth as gold." Second, He allows temptation so that we may be kept humble and utterly dependent upon Him for grace and strength to overcome the temptations. This was the apostle Paul's experience in 2 Corinthians 12:7: "And lest I should be exalted above measure through the abundance of the revelations, there was given to me a thorn in the flesh, the messenger of Satan to buffet me, lest I should be exalted above measure." Third, God permits us to be tempted so that we may be able to encourage and comfort those who are undergoing temptations. Remember that Christ Himself was tempted in all points like as we are, yet without sin, so that as our Great High Priest, He can be touched by our infirmities and help us in times of temptations (Hebrews 4:14-16). And in 2 Corinthians 1:4 Paul wrote that, God "comforteth us in all our tribulation, that we may be able to comfort them which are in any trouble" Finally, the many trials and temptations that we face in this world should make us long even more for our heavenly home where we shall finally be freed from all temptations.

SARAH: Let's talk about the third and final part of the Lord's Prayer, its conclusion. **What doth the conclusion of the Lord's prayer teach us?**

JON: **The conclusion of the Lord's prayer, (which is, For thine is the kingdom, and the power, and the glory, for ever, Amen.) teacheth us, to take our encouragement in prayer from God only, and in our**

prayers to praise him, ascribing kingdom, power, and glory to him. And in testimony of our desire, and assurance to be heard, we say, Amen. Very briefly, we learn three things from the conclusion to the Lord's Prayer. First, we find our encouragement to pray, not from ourselves, but from the very nature and character of God Himself. He is a most wise, most sovereign, most powerful, most glorious, most gracious, and most merciful God. And the best part of all is that this great God is both willing and able to answer our prayers! Second, we learn that we should praise God and ascribe all the glory to Him when we pray. Finally, when we conclude our prayers, we end with the word "amen" (meaning "may it be so") as a testimony of our desire and assurance that our heavenly Father will hear us.

TOM: Well Jon, it looks like we've come full circle. I still remember very clearly our conversation that night after driving back from Glasgow. We were talking about man's chief end and about glorifying God. Now, more than half a year later, we're rounding up our discussion on the theme of God's glory again.

JON: I'm glad to hear that you haven't forgotten that conversation we had. But I'm even happier to know that through these past few months, you've come to embrace Christ as your Saviour and Lord. Well, may God be with us and bless us as we press on in this Christian journey. Amen.

For Further Reading

Reymond, Robert L. *A New Systematic Theology of the Christian Faith*. Nashville: Thomas Nelson Publishers, 1998.

Sproul, R. C. *The Truth of the Cross*. Lake Mary, FL: Reformation Trust Publishing, 2007.

Vincent, Thomas. *The Shorter Catechism Explained from Scripture*. Edinburgh: The Banner of Truth Trust, 1980.

Watson, Thomas. *A Body of Divinity*. Edinburgh: The Banner of Truth Trust, 1997.

_____. *The Lord's Prayer*. Edinburgh: The Banner of Truth Trust, 1993.

_____. *The Ten Commandments*. Edinburgh: The Banner of Truth Trust, 1995.

Williamson. G. I. *The Shorter Catechism Volume 1&2*. Phillipsburg, NJ: Presbyterian And Reformed Publishing Co., 1970.

The Westminster Shorter Catechism with Scripture Proofs

WSC 1. **What is the chief end of man?**

A. Man's chief end is to **glorify God**,[1] and to **enjoy Him for ever**.[2]

[1]1 Cor 10:31; Rom 11:36; [2]Ps 73:25–28; Rev 7:15.

WSC 2. What rule hath God given to direct us how we may glorify and enjoy Him?

A. The **word of God**, which is contained in the Scriptures of the Old and New Testaments,[1] is the **only rule** to direct us how we may glorify and enjoy Him.[2]

[1]2 Tim 3:16; [2]1 John 1:3–4.

WSC 3. What do the Scriptures principally teach?

A. The Scriptures principally teach **what man is to believe concerning God**, and **what duty God requires of man**.[1]

[1]2 Tim 1:13; 3:16; John 5:39.

CATECHISM IN CONVERSATION

WSC 4. What is God?

A. God is a **Spirit**,[1] *infinite*,[2] *eternal*,[3] and *unchangeable*,[4] in His being,[5] wisdom,[6] power,[7] holiness,[8] justice, goodness, and truth.[9]

[1]John 4:24; [2]Job 11:7–9; [3]Ps 90:2; [4]James 1:17; [5]Exod 3:14; [6]Ps 147:5; [7]Rev 4:8; [8]Rev 15:4; [9]Exod 34:6–7.

WSC 5. Are there more Gods than one?

A. There is but **one only**, the living and true God.[1]

[1]Deut 6:4; Jer 10:10.

WSC 6. How many persons are there in the Godhead?

A. There are *three* persons in the Godhead, the *Father*, the *Son*, and the *Holy Ghost*; and these three are **one God**, the same in substance, equal in power and glory.[1]

[1]1 John 5:7; Matt 28:19.

WSC 7. What are the decrees of God?

A. The decrees of God are, **His eternal purpose**, according to the counsel of His will, whereby, for his own glory, He hath *fore-ordained* whatsoever comes to pass.[1]

[1]Eph 1:4, 11; Rom 9:22–23.

WSC 8. How doth God execute his decrees?

A. God executeth His decrees in the works of **creation** and **providence**.

WSC 9. What is the work of creation?

A. The work of creation is, God's making **all things of nothing**, by the *word* of His power, in the space of *six days*, and all *very good*.[1]

[1]Gen 1; Heb 11:3.

WSC 10. How did God create man?

A. God created man, male and female, **after His own image**, in knowledge, righteousness, and holiness, with dominion over the creatures.[1]

[1]Gen 1:26–28; Col 3:10; Eph 4:24.

WSC 11. What are God's works of providence?

A. God's works of providence are, His most holy,[1] wise,[2] and powerful **preserving**[3] **and governing** all His creatures, and all their actions.[4]

[1]Ps 145:17; [2]Ps 104:24; Isa 28:29; [3]Heb 1:3; [4]Ps 103:19; Matt 10:29–31.

WSC 12. What special act of providence did God exercise toward man in the estate wherein he was created?

A. When God had created man, He entered into a **covenant of life** with him, upon condition of *perfect obedience*, forbidding him to eat of the tree of the knowledge of good and evil, upon the pain of *death*.[1]

[1]Gal 3:12; Gen 2:17.

WSC 13. Did our first parents continue in the estate wherein they were created?

A. Our first parents, being left to the freedom of their own will, **fell** from the estate wherein they were created, by *sinning against God*.[1]

[1] Gen 3:6–8, 13; Eccles 7:29.

WSC 14. What is sin?

A. Sin is any *want of conformity* unto, or *transgression* of, the Law of God.[1]

[1]1 John 3:4.

WSC 15. What was the sin whereby our first parents fell from the estate wherein they were created?

A. The sin whereby our first parents fell from the estate wherein they were created, was their **eating the forbidden fruit**.[1]

[1]Gen 3:6, 12.

WSC 16. Did all mankind fall in Adam's first transgression?

A. The covenant being made with Adam, not only for himself, but for his posterity; **all mankind**, descending from him by ordinary generation, *sinned in him*, and *fell with him*, in his first transgression.[1]

[1]Gen 2:16–17; Rom 5:12; 1 Cor 15:21–22.

WSC 17. Into what estate did the fall bring mankind?

A. The fall brought mankind into an estate of **sin** and **misery**.[1]

[1]Rom 5:12.

WSC 18. Wherein consists the sinfulness of that estate whereinto man fell?

A. The sinfulness of that estate whereinto man fell, consists in the *guilt* of Adam's first sin, the *want* of original righteousness, and the *corruption* of his whole nature, which is commonly called **Original Sin**; together with all *actual transgressions* which proceed from it.[1]

[1]Rom 5:10–20; Eph 2:1–3; James 1:14–15; Matt 15:19.

WSC 19. What is the misery of that estate whereinto man fell?

A. All mankind by their fall **lost communion with God**,[1] are under His *wrath and curse*,[2] and so made liable to *all miseries in this life*, to death itself, and to the pains of *hell* for ever.[3]

[1]Isa 59:2; Gen 3:8, 10, 24; [2]Gen 3:17; Eph 2:2–3; Gal 3:10; [3]Ezek 18:4; Ps 9:17; Rom 6:23; Matt 25:41, 46.

WSC 20. Did God leave all mankind to perish in the estate of sin and misery?

A. God having, out of his mere good pleasure, from all eternity, elected some to everlasting life,[1] did enter into a **covenant of grace**, to *deliver them* out of the estate of sin and misery, and to bring them into an estate of *salvation* by a **Redeemer**.[2]

[1]Eph 1:4; [2]Rom 3:20–22; Gal 3:21–22.

WSC 21. Who is the Redeemer of God's elect?

A. The only Redeemer of God's elect is the **Lord Jesus Christ**,[1] who, being the eternal *Son of God*, **became man**,[2] and so was, and continueth to be, *God and man* in two distinct natures, and one person, for ever.[3]

[1]1 Tim 2:5–6; [2]John 1:14; Gal 4:4; [3]Rom 9:5; Luke 1:35; Col 2:9; Heb 7:24–25.

WSC 22. How did Christ, being the Son of God, become man?

A. Christ, the Son of God, became man, by taking to himself **a true body**,[1] **and a reasonable soul**,[2] being conceived by the power of the *Holy Ghost*, in the womb of the *Virgin Mary*,[3] and born of her, yet without sin.[4]

[1]Heb 2:14, 16; 10:5; [2]Matt 26:38; [3]Luke 1:27, 31, 35, 42; Gal 4:4; [4]Heb 4:15; 7:26.

WSC 23. What offices doth Christ excecute as our Redeemer?

A. Christ, as our Redeemer, executeth the offices of a **prophet**, of a **priest**, and of a **king**, both in his estate of *humiliation* and *exaltation*.[1]

[1]Acts 3:21–22; Heb 12:25; cf. 2 Cor 13:3; Heb 5:5–7; 7:25; Ps 2:6; Isa 9:6–7; Matt 21:5; Ps 2:8–11.

WSC 24. How doth Christ execute the office of a prophet?

A. Christ executeth the office of a prophet, in *revealing* to us, by his Word and Spirit, **the will of God** for our salvation.[1]

[1]John 1:18; 1 Pet 1:10–12; John 15:15; 20:31.

WSC 25. How doth Christ execute the office of a priest?

A. Christ executeth the office of a priest, in his once *offering up of himself* **a sacrifice** to satisfy divine justice,[1] and reconcile us to God;[2] and in *making continual intercession* for us.[3]

[1]Heb 9:14, 28; [2]Heb 2:17; [3]Heb 7:24–25.

WSC 26. How doth Christ execute the office of a king?

A. Christ executeth the office of a king, in **subduing us to himself**,[1] in *ruling*[2] *and defending* us,[3] and in *restraining and conquering* all his and our enemies.[4]

[1]Acts 15:14–16; [2]Isa 33:22; [3]Isa 32:1–2; [4]1 Cor 15:25; Ps 110.

WSC 27. Wherein did Christ's humiliation consist?

A. Christ's humiliation consisted in his *being born*, and that in a *low condition*,[1] *made under the law*,[2] undergoing the *miseries of this life*,[3] the *wrath of God*,[4] and the *cursed death* of the **cross**;[5] in being *buried*,[6] and *continuing under the power of death* for a time.[7]

[1]Luke 2:7; [2]Gal 4:4; [3]Heb 12:2–3; Isa 53:2–3; [4]Luke 22:44; Matt 27:46; [5] Phil 2:8; [6]1 Cor 15:3–4; [7]Acts 2:24–27, 31.

WSC 28. Wherein consisteth Christ's exaltation?

A. Christ's exaltation consisteth in His *rising again from the dead* on the third day,[1] in *ascending up into heaven*,[2] in **sitting at the right hand of God** *the Father*,[3] and in *coming to judge the world* at the last day.[4]

[1]1 Cor 15:4; [2]Mark 16:19; [3]Eph 1:20; [4]Acts 1:11; 17:31.

WSC 29. How are we made partakers of the redemption purchased by Christ?

A. We are made partakers of the redemption purchased by Christ, by the *effectual application* of it to us[1] by **his Holy Spirit**.[2]

[1]John 1:11–12; [2]Titus 3:5–6.

WSC 30. How doth the Spirit apply to us the redemption purchased by Christ?

A. The Spirit applieth to us the redemption purchased by Christ, by working **faith** in us,[1] and thereby *uniting us to Christ* in our effectual calling.[2]

[1]Eph 1:13–14; John 6:37, 39; Eph 2:8; [2]Eph 3:17; 1 Cor 1:9.

WSC 31. What is effectual calling?

A. Effectual calling is the **work of God's Spirit**,[1] whereby, convincing us of our *sin and misery*,[2] enlightening our minds in the *knowledge of Christ*,[3] and *renewing our wills*,[4]he doth persuade and enable us to *embrace* **Jesus Christ**, freely offered to us in the gospel.[5]

[1]2 Tim 1:9; 2 Thess 2:13–14; [2]Acts 2:37; [3]Acts 26:18; [4]Ezek 36:26–27; [5]John 6:44–45; Phil 2:13.

WSC 32. What benefits do they that are effectually called partake of in this life?

A. They that are effectually called do in this life partake of **justification**,[1] **adoption**,[2] and **sanctification**, and *the several benefits* which in this life do either accompany or flow from them.[3]

[1]Rom 8:30; [2]Eph 1:5; [3]1 Cor 1:26, 30.

WSC 33. What is justification?

A. Justification is *an act of God's free grace*, wherein he *pardoneth all our sins*,[1] and *accepteth us as righteous* in His sight,[2] only for the **righteousness of Christ** imputed to us,[3] and received by *faith* alone.[4]

[1]Rom 3:24–25; 4:6–8; [2]2 Cor 5:19, 21; [3]Rom 5:17–19; [4]Gal 2:16; Phil 3:9.

WSC 34. What is adoption?

A. Adoption is *an act of God's free grace*,[1] whereby we are *received into the number*, and *have a right to all the privileges* of the **sons of God**.[2]

[1]1 John 3:1; [2]John 1:12; Rom 8:17.

WSC 35. What is sanctification?

A. Sanctification is *the work of God's free grace*,[1] whereby we are renewed in the whole man after the **image of God**,[2] and are enabled more and more to *die unto sin*, and *live unto righteousness*.[3]

[1]2 Thess 2:13; [2]Eph 4:23–24; [3]Rom 6:4, 6; 8:1.

WSC 36. What are the benefits which in this life do accompany or flow from justification, adoption, and sanctification?

A. The benefits which in this life do accompany or flow from justification, adoption, and sanctification, are, *assurance of God's love, peace of conscience*,[1] *joy in the Holy Ghost*,[2] *increase of grace*,[3] and *perseverance* therein to the end.[4]

[1]Rom 5:1–2, 5; [2]Rom 14:17; [3]Prov 4:18; [4]1 John 5:13; 1 Pet 1:5.

WSC 37. What benefits do believers receive from Christ at death?

A. The *souls* of believers are at their death made *perfect in holiness*,[1] and do immediately **pass into glory**;[2] and their *bodies*, being still *united to Christ*,[3] do rest in their graves[4] till the resurrection.[5]

[1]Heb 12:23; [2]2 Cor 5:1, 6, 8; Phil 1:23; Luke 23:43; [3]1 Thess 4:14; [4]Isa 57:2; [5]Job 19:26–27.

WSC 38. What benefits do believers receive from Christ at the resurrection?

A. At the resurrection, believers being *raised up in glory*,[1] shall be o*penly acknowledged and acquitted* in the day of judgment,[2] and made perfectly blessed in the full **enjoying of God**[3] to all eternity.[4]

[1]1 Cor 15:43; [2]Matt 25:23; 10:32; [3]1 John 3:2; 1 Cor 13:12; [4]1 Thess 4:17.

WSC 39. What is the duty which God requireth of man?

A. The duty which God requireth of man, is **obedience to His revealed will.**[1]

[1]Mic 6:8; 1 Sam 15:22.

WSC 40. What did God at first reveal to man for the rule of his obedience?

A. The rule which God at first revealed to man for his obedience, was **the moral law.**[1]

[1]Rom 2:14–15; 10:5.

WSC 41. Where is the moral law summarily comprehended?

A. The moral law is summarily comprehended in **the ten commandments**.[1]

[1]Deut 10:4; Matt 19:17.

WSC 42. What is the sum of the Ten Commandments?

A. The sum of the Ten Commandments is, **To love the Lord our God** with all our heart, with all our soul, with all our strength, and with all our mind; and **our neighbour** as ourselves.[1]

[1]Matt 22:37–40; Mark 12:30–31.

WSC 43. What is the preface to the ten commandments?

A. The preface to the ten commandments is in these words, **I am the Lord thy God, which have brought thee out of the land of Egypt, out of the house of bondage.**[1]

[1]Exod 20:2; Deut 5:6.

WSC 44. What doth the preface to the ten commandments teach us?

A. The preface to the ten commandments teacheth us, That because God is **the Lord**, and **our God**, and **Redeemer**, therefore we are bound to keep all his commandments.[1]

[1]Luke 1:74–75; 1 Pet 1:15–19.

CATECHISM WITH SCRIPTURE PROOFS

WSC 45. Which is the first commandment?

A. The first commandment is, **Thou shalt have no other gods before me.**[1]

[1]Exod 20:3.

WSC 46. What is required in the first commandment?

A. The first commandment requireth us to *know* and *acknowledge* God to be the only *true* God, and *our* God,[1] and to *worship* and *glorify* Him accordingly.[2]

[1]1 Chron 28:9; Deut 26:17; [2]Matt 4:10; Ps 29:2.

WSC 47. What is forbidden in the first commandment?

A. The first commandment forbiddeth the *denying*,[1] or *not worshipping and glorifying* the true God as God,[2] and our God;[3] and the giving of that worship and glory *to any other*, which is due to him alone.[4]

[1]Ps 14:1; [2]Rom 1:21; [3]Ps 81:10–11; [4]Rom 1:25.

WSC 48. What are we specially taught by these words "before me" in the first commandment?

A. These words "**before me**," in the first commandment, teach us, That God, who seeth all things, *taketh notice of*, and is *much displeased with*, the sin of **having any other god**.[1]

[1]Rom 1:20–21; Ps 44:20–21; Ezek 8:5–18.

WSC 49. Which is the second commandment?

A. The second commandment is, **Thou shalt not make unto thee any graven image**, or any likeness of any thing that is in heaven above, or that is in the earth beneath, or that is in the water under the earth: **Thou shalt not bow down thyself to them**, nor serve them: for I the Lord thy God am a *jealous* God, visiting the iniquity of the fathers upon the children unto the third and fourth generation of them that hate me; and shewing mercy unto thousands of them that love me, and keep my commandments.[1]

[1]Exod 20:4–6.

WSC 50. What is required in the second commandment?

A. The second commandment requireth the receiving, observing, and keeping pure and entire, *all such religious worship and ordinances as God hath appointed* in His Word.[1]

[1]Deut 32:46; Matt 28:20; Acts 2:42.

WSC 51. What is forbidden in the second commandment?

A. The second commandment forbiddeth the worshipping of God by *images*,[1] *or any other way not appointed in his word.*[2]

[1]Deut 4:15–19; Exod 32:5, 8; [2]Deut 12:31–32.

WSC 52. What are the reasons annexed to the second commandment?

A. The reasons annexed to the second commandment are,

God's *sovereignty* over us,[1] his *propriety* in us,[2] and the *zeal* he hath to his own worship.[3]

[1]Ps 95:2–3, 6; [2]Ps 45:11; [3]Exod 34:13–14.

WSC 53. Which is the third commandment?

A. The third commandment is, **Thou shalt not take the name of the Lord thy God in vain**: for the Lord will not hold him guiltless that taketh his name in vain.[1]

[1]Exod 20:7.

WSC 54. What is required in the third commandment?

A. The third commandment requireth *the holy and reverend use* of God's names,[1] titles,[2] attributes,[3] ordinances,[4] word[5] and works.[6]

[1]Matt 6:9; Deut 28:58; [2]Ps 68:4; [3]Rev 15:3–4; [4]Mal 1:11, 14; [5]Ps 138:1–2; [6]Job 36:24.

WSC 55. What is forbidden in the third commandment?

A. The third commandment forbiddeth all *profaning* or *abusing* of any thing whereby God maketh Himself known.[1]

[1]Mal 1:6–7, 12; 2:2; 3:14.

WSC 56. What is the reason annexed to the third commandment?

A. The reason annexed to the third commandment is, That however the breakers of this commandment may escape punishment from *men*, yet **the Lord our God** will not suffer them to escape His righteous judgment.[1]

[1]1 Sam 2:12, 17, 22, 29; 3:13; Deut 28:58–59.

WSC 57. Which is the fourth commandment?

A. The fourth commandment is, **Remember the Sabbath day, to keep it holy**. *Six days* shalt thou, labour, and do all thy work: but the *seventh day* is the **Sabbath** of the Lord thy God: in it **thou shalt not do any work**, thou, nor thy son, nor thy daughter, thy man-servant, nor thy maid-servant, nor thy cattle, nor thy stranger that is within thy gates: for in *six days* the Lord made heaven and earth, the sea, and all that in them is, and *rested the seventh day*: wherefore the Lord *blessed* the Sabbath day, and *hallowed* it.[1]

[1]Exod 20:8–11.

WSC 58. What is required in the fourth commandment?

A. The fourth commandment requireth the keeping holy to God *such set times as he hath appointed in his Word*; expressly *one whole day in seven*, to be a holy Sabbath to himself.[1]

[1]Deut 5:12–14.

WSC 59. Which day of the seven hath God appointed to be the weekly Sabbath?

A. From the beginning of the world to the resurrection of Christ, God appointed the *seventh* day of the week to be the weekly Sabbath; and the *first* day of the week ever since, to continue to the end of the world, which is the **Christian** Sabbath.[1]

[1]Gen 2:2–3; 1 Cor 16:1–2; Acts 20:7.

WSC 60. How is the Sabbath to be sanctified?

A. The Sabbath is to be sanctified by a holy **resting** all that day,[1] even from such worldly employments and recreations as are lawful on *other* days;[2] and spending the whole time in the *public and private exercises of God's worship,*[3] except so much as is to be taken up in the works of **necessity** and **mercy**.[4]

[1]Exod 20:8, 10; 16:25–28; [2]Neh 13:15–22; [3]Luke 4:16; Acts 20:7; Ps 92 title; Isa 66:23; [4]Matt 12:1–31.

WSC 61. What is forbidden in the fourth commandment?

A. The fourth commandment forbiddeth the *omission or careless performance* of the duties required,[1] and the profaning the day by *idleness,*[2] or doing that which is in itself *sinful,*[3] or by unnecessary thoughts, words, or works, about our *worldly* employments or recreations.[4]

[1]Ezek 22:26; Amos 8:5; Mal 1:13; [2]Acts 20:7, 9; [3]Ezek 23:38; [4]Jer 17:24–26; Isa 58:13.

WSC 62. What are the reasons annexed to the fourth commandment?

A. The reasons annexed to the fourth commandment are, God's allowing us *six* days of the week for our own employments,[1] his challenging a special propriety in the *seventh*, his own *example*, and his *blessing* the Sabbath day.[2]

[1]Exod 20:9; [2]Exod 20:11.

WSC 63. Which is the fifth commandment?

A. The fifth commandment is, **Honour thy father and thy mother**; that thy days may be *long* upon the land which the Lord thy God giveth thee.[1]

[1]Exod 20:12.

WSC 64. What is required in the fifth commandment?

A. The fifth commandment requireth the *preserving the honour*, and *performing the duties*, belonging to *every one* in their several places and relations, as superiors,[1] inferiors,[2] or equals.[3]

[1]Eph 5:21; [2]1 Pet. 2:17; [3]Rom 12:10.

WSC 65. What is forbidden in the fifth commandment?

A. The fifth commandment forbiddeth the *neglecting of*, or *doing any thing against*, the honour and duty which belongeth to every one in their several places and relations.[1]

[1]Matt 15:4–6; Ezek 34:2–4; Rom 13:8.

WSC 66. What is the reason annexed to the fifth commandment?

A. The reason annexed to the fifth commandment, is *a*

promise of long life and prosperity (as far as it shall serve for God's glory and their own good) to all such as keep this commandment.[1]

[1]Deut 5:16; Eph 6:2–3.

WSC 67. Which is the sixth commandment?

A. The sixth commandment is, **Thou shalt not kill**.[1]

[1]Ex 20:13.

WSC 68. What is required in the sixth commandment?

A. The sixth commandment requireth all lawful endeavours to *preserve* our own life,[1] and the life of others.[2]

[1]Eph 5:28–29; [2]1 Kings 18:4.

WSC 69. What is forbidden in the sixth commandment?

A. The sixth commandment forbiddeth the *taking away* of our own life, or the life of our neighbour unjustly, or whatsoever *tendeth* thereunto.[1]

[1]Acts 16:28; Gen 9:6.

WSC 70. Which is the seventh commandment?

A. The seventh commandment is, **Thou shalt not commit adultery**.[1]

[1]Exod 20:14.

WSC 71. What is required in the seventh commandment?

A. The seventh commandment requireth the preservation of our own and our neighbour's *chastity*, in heart, speech, and behaviour.[1]

[1]1 Cor 7:2–3, 5, 34, 36; Col 4:6; 1 Pet. 3:2.

WSC 72. What is forbidden in the seventh commandment?

A. The seventh commandment forbiddeth *all unchaste* thoughts, words, and actions.[1]

[1]Matt 15:19; 5:28; Eph 5:3–4.

WSC 73. Which is the eighth commandment?

A. The eighth commandment is, **Thou shalt not steal.**[1]

[1]Exod 20:15.

WSC 74. What is required in the eighth commandment?

A. The eighth commandment requireth the *lawful procuring and furthering* the wealth and outward estate of ourselves and others.[1]

[1]Gen 30:30; 1 Tim 5:8; Lev 25:35; Deut 22:1–5; Exod 23:4–5; Gen 47:14, 20.

WSC 75. What is forbidden in the eighth commandment?

A. The eighth commandment forbiddeth whatsoever doth or may unjustly *hinder* our own or our neighbour's wealth or outward estate.[1]

[1]Prov 21:17; 23:20–21; 28:19; Eph 4:28.

WSC 76. Which is the ninth commandment?

A. The ninth commandment is, **Thou shalt not bear false witness against thy neighbour.**[1]

[1]Exod 20:16.

WSC 77. What is required in the ninth commandment?

A. The ninth commandment requireth the maintaining and promoting of *truth* between man and man,[1] and of our own and our neighbour's *good name*,[2] especially in witness-bearing.[3]

[1]Zech 8:16; [2]3 John 12; [3]Prov 14:5, 25.

WSC 78. What is forbidden in the ninth commandment?

A. The ninth commandment forbiddeth whatsoever is *prejudicial* to truth, or *injurious* to our own or our neighbour's good name.[1]

[1]1 Sam 17:28; Lev 19:16; Ps 15:3.

WSC 79. Which is the tenth commandment?

A. The tenth commandment is, **Thou shalt not covet** thy neighbour's *house*, thou shalt not covet thy neighbour's *wife*, nor his *man-servant*, nor his *maid-servant*, nor his *ox*, nor his *ass*, nor *any thing* that is thy neighbour's.[1]

[1]Exod 20:17.

WSC 80. What is required in the tenth commandment?

A. The tenth commandment requireth full *contentment* with our own condition,[1] with a *right and charitable frame of* *spirit* toward our neighbour, and all that is his.[2]

[1]Heb 13:5; 1 Tim 6:6; [2]Job 31:29; Rom 12:15; 1 Tim 1:5; 1 Cor 13:4–7.

WSC 81. What is forbidden in the tenth commandment?

A. The tenth commandment forbiddeth all *discontentment* with our own estate,[1] *envying or grieving* at the good of our neighbour,[2] and all *inordinate* motions and affections to any thing that is his.[3]

[1]1 Kings 21:4; Esther 5:13; 1 Cor 10:10; [2]Gal 5:26; James 3:14, 16; [3]Rom 7:7–8; 13:9; Deut 5:21.

WSC 82. Is any man able perfectly to keep the commandments of God?

A. No *mere* man since the fall is able in *this* life **perfectly** to keep the commandments of God,[1] but doth *daily* break them in thought, word, and deed.[2]

[1]Eccles 7:20; 1 John 1:8, 10; Gal 5:17; [2]Gen 6:5; 8:21; Rom 3:9–21; James 3:2–13.

WSC 83. Are all transgressions of the law equally heinous?

A. Some sins *in themselves*, and by reason of several *aggravations*, are **more heinous** in the sight of God than others.[1]

[1]Ezek 8:6, 13, 15; 1 John 5:16; Ps 78:17, 32, 56.

WSC 84. What doth every sin deserve?

A. Every sin deserveth God's **wrath and curse**, both in *this* life, and that which *is to come*.[1]

[1]Eph 5:6; Gal 3:10; Lam 3:39; Matt 25:41.

WSC 85. What doth God require of us, that we may escape his wrath and curse due to us for sin?

A. To escape the wrath and curse of God due to us for sin, God requireth of us **faith in Jesus Christ**, **repentance unto life**,[1] with the diligent use of all the **outward means** whereby Christ communicateth to us the benefits of redemption.[2]

[1]Acts 20:21; [2]Prov 2:1–5; 8:33–36; Isa 55:3.

WSC 86. What is Faith in Jesus Christ?

A. Faith in Jesus Christ is a *saving grace*,[1] whereby we **receive** and **rest upon Him alone** for salvation, as he is offered to us in the gospel.[2]

[1]Heb 10:39; [2]John 1:12; Isa 26:3–4; Phil 3:9; Gal 2:16.

WSC 87. What is repentance unto Life?

A. Repentance unto life is a *saving grace*,[1] whereby a sinner, out of a *true sense of his sin*,[2] and apprehension of the *mercy of God in Christ*,[3] doth, with grief and hatred of his sin, **turn from it unto God**,[4] with full purpose of, and endeavour after, *new obedience*.[5]

[1]Acts 11:18; [2]Acts 2:37–38; [3]Joel 2:12; Jer 3:22; [4]Jer 31:18–19; Ezek 36:31; [5]2 Cor 7:11.

WSC 88. What are the outward means whereby Christ communicateth to us the benefits of redemption?

A. The outward and ordinary means whereby Christ communicateth to us the benefits of redemption, are **his ordinances**, especially the *Word*, *sacraments*, and *prayer*; all which are made effectual to the elect for salvation.[1]

[1]Matt 28:19–20; Acts 2:42, 46–47.

WSC 89. How is the word made effectual to salvation?

A. The Spirit of God maketh the *reading*, but especially the *preaching*, of the word, an effectual means of *convincing* and *converting* sinners, and of *building them up* in holiness and comfort, through faith, unto salvation.[1]

[1]Neh 8:8; 1 Cor 14:24–25; Acts 26:18; Ps 19:8; Acts 20:32; Rom 15:4; 2 Tim 3:15–17; Rom 10:13–17; 1:16.

WSC 90. How is the word to be read and heard, that it may become effectual to salvation?

A. That the word may become effectual to salvation, we must attend thereunto with *diligence*,[1] *preparation*,[2] and *prayer*;[3] receive it with *faith and love*,[4] lay it up in our *hearts*,[5] and practise it in our *lives*.[6]

[1]Prov 8:34; [2]1 Pet 2:1–2; [3]Ps 119:18; [4]Heb 4:2; 2 Thess 2:10; [5] Ps 119:11; [6]Luke 8:15; James 1:25.

WSC 91. How do the sacraments become effectual means of salvation?

A. The sacraments become effectual means of salvation, not from any *virtue* in them, or in him that doth administer them; but only by the **blessing of Christ**,[1] and the **working of his Spirit** in them that by faith receive them.[2]

[1]1 Pet 3:21; Matt 3:11; 1 Cor 3:6–7; [2]1 Cor 12:13.

WSC 92. What is a sacrament?

A. A sacrament is an holy *ordinance* instituted by **Christ**; wherein, *by sensible signs*, Christ, and the benefits of the new covenant, are represented, sealed, and applied to believers.[1]

[1]Gen 17:7, 10; Exod 12; 1 Cor 11:23, 26.

WSC 93. Which are the sacraments of the New Testament?

A. The sacraments of the New Testament are, *Baptism*,[1] and the *Lord's Supper*.[2]

[1]Matt 28:19; [2]Matt 26:26–28.

WSC 94. What is baptism?

A. Baptism is a sacrament, wherein the *washing with water* in the name of the Father, and of the Son, and of the Holy Ghost,[1] doth signify and seal our *ingrafting into Christ*, and *partaking of the benefits* of the covenant of grace, and our *engagement* to be the Lord's.[2]

[1]Matt 28:19; [2]Rom 6:4; Gal 3:27.

WSC 95. To whom is baptism to be administered?

A. Baptism is *not* to be administered to any that are out of the visible church, *till they profess their faith in Christ*, and *obedience* to Him;[1] but the *infants of such as are members* of the visible church are to be baptised.[2]

[1]Acts 8:36–37; 2:38; [2]Acts 2:38–39; Gen 17:10; cf. Col 2:11–12; 1 Cor 7:14.

WSC 96. What is the Lord's Supper?

A. The Lord's Supper is a sacrament, wherein, by giving and *receiving bread and wine, according to Christ's appointment*, his **death** is shewed forth; and the worthy receivers are, not after a corporal and carnal manner, but *by faith*, made partakers of his *body and blood*, with all his benefits, to their spiritual nourishment, and growth in grace.[1]

[1]1 Cor 11:23–26; 10:16.

WSC 97. What is required to the worthy receiving of the Lord's supper?

A. It is required of them that would worthily partake of the Lord's supper, that they examine themselves of their *knowledge to discern the Lord's body*,[1] of their *faith to feed upon Him*,[2] of their *repentance*,[3] *love*,[4] and *new obedience*;[5] lest, coming unworthily, they eat and drink judgment to themselves.[6]

[1]1 Cor 11:28–29; [2]2 Cor 13:5; [3]1 Cor 11:31; [4]1 Cor

10:16–17; [5]1Cor 5:7–8; [6]1 Cor 11:28–29.

WSC 98. What is prayer?

A. Prayer is an offering up of our desires unto God,[1] for things *agreeable to His will,*[2] in the name of **Christ,**[3] with confession of *our sins,*[4] and thankful acknowledgment of *His mercies.*[5]

[1]Ps 62:8; [2]1 John 5:14; [3]John 16:23; [4]Ps 32:5–6; Dan 9:4; [5]Phil 4:6.

WSC 99. What rule hath God given for our direction in prayer?

A. The *whole word of God* is of use to direct us in prayer;[1] but the *special* rule of direction is that form of prayer which Christ taught his disciples, commonly called The **Lord's Prayer.**[2]

[1]1 John 5:14; [2]Matt 6:9–13 cf. Luke 11:2–4.

WSC 100. What doth the preface of the Lord's prayer teach us?

A. The preface of the Lord's prayer, (which is, **Our Father which art in heaven,**[1]) teacheth us to draw near to God with all holy *reverence* and *confidence,* as children to a father, able and ready to help us;[2]and that we should pray *with* and *for* others.[3]

[1]Matt 6:9; [2]Rom 8:15; Luke 11:13; [3]Acts 12:5; 1 Tim 2:1–2.

WSC 101. What do we pray for in the first petition?

A. In the first petition, (which is, **Hallowed be thy name,**[1]) we pray, That God would enable us and others to *glorify* him in all that whereby he maketh himself known;[2]—and that he would dispose all things to his own glory.[3]

[1]Mt 6:9; [2]Ps 67:2–3; [3]Ps 83.

WSC 102. What do .we pray for in the second petition?

A. In the second petition, (which is, **Thy kingdom come,**[1]) we pray, That *Satan's kingdom* may be destroyed;[2] and that the *kingdom of Grace* may be advanced,[3] ourselves and others brought into it, and kept in it;[4] and that the *kingdom of Glory* may be hastened.[5]

[1]Matt 6:10; [2]Ps 68:1, 18; [3]Rev 12:10–11; [4]2 Thess 3:1; Rom 10:1; John 17:9, 20; [5]Rev 22:20.

WSC 103. What do we pray for in the third petition?

A. In the third petition, (which is, **Thy will be done in earth, as it is in heaven,**[1]) we pray, That God, by his grace, would make us able and willing to *know, obey,* and *submit to his will* in all things,[2] as the angels do in heaven.[3]

[1]Matt 6:10; [2]Ps 67; 119:36; Matt 26:39; 2 Sam 15:25; Job 1:21; [3]Ps 103:20–21.

WSC 104. What do we pray for in the fourth petition?

A. In the fourth petition, (which is, **Give us this day our daily bread,**[1]) we pray, That of God's free gift we may receive a *competent portion* of the good things of this life, and enjoy *his blessing* with them.[2]

[1]Matt 6:11; [2]Prov 30:8–9; Gen 28:20; 1 Tim 4:4–5.

WSC 105. What do we pray for in the fifth petition?

A. In the fifth petition, (which is, **And forgive us our debts, as we forgive our debtors,**[1]) we pray, That God, for Christ's sake, would freely *pardon all our sins*;[2] which we are the rather encouraged to ask, because by his grace we are enabled from the heart to *forgive others*.[3]

[1]Matt 6:12; [2]Ps 51:1–2, 7, 9; Dan 9:17–19; [3]Luke 11:4; Matt 18:35.

WSC 106. What do we pray for in the sixth petition?

A. In the sixth petition, (which is, **And lead us not into temptation, but deliver us from evil,**[1]) we pray, That God would *either keep us* from being tempted to sin,[2] or *support and deliver us* when we *are* tempted.[3]

[1]Matt 6:13; [2]Matt 26:41; [3]2 Cor 12:7–8.

WSC 107. What doth the conclusion of the Lord's prayer teach us?

A. The conclusion of the Lord's prayer, (which is, **For thine is the kingdom, and the power, and the glory, for ever, Amen.**[1]) teacheth us to take our encouragement in prayer from **God only**,[2] and in our prayers to *praise* him, ascribing kingdom, power, and glory to him.[3] And, in testimony of our *desire*, and *assurance* to be heard, we say, Amen.[4]

[1]Matt 6:13; [2]Dan 9:4, 7–9, 16–19; [3]1 Chron 29:10–13; [4]1 Cor 14:16; Rev 22:20–21.

Notes

[1] Besides those books I have listed under For Further Reading, I have also added notes along the way, pointing out where the reader can turn for more material on selected topics.

[2] For more on glorifying God, see Thomas Watson, *A Body of Divinity* (Edinburgh: The Banner of Truth Trust, 1997), 7-20.

[3] For more on enjoying God, see ibid., 20-26.

[4] An excellent book on the subject of "chance" is R. C. Sproul, *Not a Chance* (Grand Rapids: Baker Books, 1994).

[5] For more on this question of how we may know that the Bible is God's inspired Word, see Gordon H. Clark, *God's Hammer: The Bible and Its Critics* (Hobbs, New Mexico: The Trinity Foundation, 1982), 1-23.

[6] For a very helpful devotional commentary on the Gospel according to Luke, see R. C. Sproul, *A Walk with Jesus* (Geanies House, Fearn, Ross-Shire, Scotland: Christian Focus Publications, 1999).

[7] For a very helpful analysis of the Shorter Catechism definition of God, see Robert L. Reymond, *A New Systematic Theology of the Christian Faith* (Nashville: Thomas Nelson Publishers, 1998), 164-202

[8] For a thoroughly readable book on the Trinity, see Stuart Olyott, *The Three Are One* (Darlington, Durham: Evangelical Press, 1996).

[9] A useful discussion on "why God is not the author or chargeable cause of sin" can be found in Reymond, *A New Systematic Theology of the Christian Faith,* 372-76.

[10] For more on the question of the literal days of creation, see Kenneth L. Gentry, Jr., *Nourishment from the Word* (Ventura, CA: Nordskog Publishing, 2008), 91-99.

[11] My favourite book on predestination is R. C. Sproul's *Chosen by God* (Wheaton, IL: Tyndale House Publishers, 1986). Highly Recommended!

[12] Taken from the Scottish Metrical Version of the Psalms (1650).

[13] For a very helpful book on the person and work of Jesus Christ, see Joseph A. Pipa, *The Root & Branch* (Geanies House, Fearn, Ross-Shire, Scotland: Christian Focus Publications, 1989).

[14] John Bunyan, *The Works of John Bunyan* (Edinburgh: The Banner of Truth Trust, 1991), 1:521.

[15] John Bunyan, *The Pilgrim's Progress* (Penguin Classics, 1987).

[16] Joseph Alleine, *A Sure Guide to Heaven* (Edinburgh: The Banner of Truth Trust, 1995).

[17] For a good introduction to this difficult doctrine of justification, see *Justification by Faith ALONE* (Morgan, PA: Soli Deo Gloria Publications, 1995).

[18] For an introduction to the relationship between faith and works, see Rev. Don Kistler, ed., *Trust and Obey*

(Obedience and the Christian) (Morgan, PA: Soli Deo Gloria Publications, 1996).

[19] Thomas Watson, *The Ten Commandments* (Edinburgh: The Banner of Truth Trust, 1995), 1.

[20] For more on the ceremonial and judicial laws, see Gentry, *Nourishment from the Word*, 116-24.

[21] Adapted from the Westminster Larger Catechism, Q. 104.

[22] Christians today have largely neglected God's divinely inspired hymnbook for the church, i.e., the book of Psalms. A good place to start reading on this subject is Brian M. Schwertley, *Exclusive Psalmody* (Saunderstown, RI: The American Presbyterian Press, 2002).

[23] Watson, *The Ten Commandments* (Edinburgh: The Banner of Truth Trust, 1995), 60.

[24] Illustration taken from James Beeke, *Bible Doctrine for Older Children, Book B* (The Netherlands Reformed Book and Publishing Committee, 2004), 99.

[25] A great place to start reading on the fourth commandment is Joseph A. Pipa, *The Lord's Day* (Geanies House, Fearn, Ross-Shire, Scotland: Christian Focus, 1997).

[26] I've found Maurice Roberts's *The Thought of God* (Edinburgh: The Banner of Truth Trust, 1995) and *The Christian's High Calling* (Edinburgh: The Banner of Truth Trust, 2000) very suitable for reading on the Sabbath.

[27] Thomas Vincent, *The Shorter Catechism Explained from Scripture* (Edinburgh: The Banner of Truth Trust, 1980), 152.

[28] Illustration taken from Beeke, *Bible Doctrine for Older Children, Book B,* 134.

[29] Richard Baxter, *A Christian Directory* (Morgan, PA: Soli Deo Gloria Publications, 1996), 248.

[30] Illustration adapted from Beeke, *Bible Doctrine for Older Children, Book B,* 134.

[31] Arthur W. Pink, *The Ten Commandments* (Grand Rapids: Baker Books, 1994).

[32] Saint Augustine, *Confessions* (Penguin Books, 1961), 21.

[33] Illustration taken from Beeke, *Bible Doctrine for Older Children, Book B,* 42.

[34] Thomas Watson, *The Doctrine of Repentance* (Edinburgh: The Banner of Truth Trust, 1994), 7.

[35] Obadiah Sedgwick, *Christ's Counsel to His Languishing Church* (Morgan, PA: Soli Deo Gloria Publications, 1996), chapter 1.

[36] Louis Berkhof, *Systematic Theology* (Edinburgh: The Banner of Truth Trust, 1994), 616.

[37] Thomas Vincent, *The Shorter Catechism Explained from Scripture* (Edinburgh: The Banner of Truth Trust, 1980), 244.

[38] A helpful place to start on this topic of baptism is Rodger M. Crooks, *Salvation's Sign and Seal* (Geanies House, Fearn, Ross-Shire, Scotland: Christian Focus Publications, 1997).

[39] For a discussion on the relationship between circumcision in the Old Testament and baptism in the New Testament, see O. Palmer Robertson, *The Christ of the Covenants* (Phillipsburg, NJ: P&R Publishing, 1980), 147-66.

[40] *The Puritans on the Lord's Supper* (Morgan, PA: Soli Deo Gloria Publications, 1997), 2.

[41] For an excellent book on the Lord's Supper and, in particular, on how Christ is present in the Supper, please see Keith A. Mathison, *Given for You* (Phillipsburg, NJ: P&R Publishing Company, 2002).

[42] *The Puritans on The Lord's Supper,* 120.

[43] Ibid., chapter 5.

[44] Jonathan Edwards, ed., *The Life and Diary of David Brainerd* (Grand Rapids: Baker Books, 1989), 365.

[45] Thomas Watson, *The Lord's Prayer* (Edinburgh: The Banner of Truth Trust, 1993), 62.

[46] Arthur W. Pink, *The Sovereignty of God* (Grand Rapids: Baker Books, 1997), 172, 176.

[47] Matthew Henry, *Commentary on the Whole Bible* (Peabody, MA: Hendrickson Publishers, 1991), 1638.

About the Author

Linus Chua is a member of Pilgrim Covenant Church in Singapore and a full-time ministerial student under the care of the church session. He was born August 1, 1974 in Singapore and is married to Shan Shan. They have three young children: Rebekah, Euan, and Luke.

After graduating from Imperial College London (UK) in 1999 with a M.Eng in aeronautical engineering, Linus worked as an aeronautical engineer for five and a half years at DSO National Laboratories. He is currently pursuing the M.Div. degree with Whitefield Theological Seminary in preparation for the pastoral ministry.

Linus has written a book, *Not to Destroy, But to Fulfill*, in which he gives an exposition of Christ's teaching on the law in the Sermon on the Mount (Matt. 5:17-48).

If you would like to contact him, you may do so at linuschua74@yahoo.com.